ROOMANITARIAN

HENRY ROLLINS

2.31.61 Publications, Inc.

Roomanitarian © 2005 Henry Rollins

Thanks: Carol Bua, Heidi May, Mike Curtis, Richard Bishop,
Mitch Bury of Adams Mass.

Layout and design by Dave Chapple, www.chappledesign.com

For Ginger, always.

JOE COLE 4.10.61 – 12.19.91

2.13.61 Publcations, Inc.

2.13.61
7510 Sunset Blvd. #602
Los Angeles, CA 90046
www.21361.com
www.henryrollins.com

Ended

Sometimes I light fires. Not because I have a thing for fire. Not because I like the smell of a wood burning. Not because it makes me think of autumn, or the cooling of the air, or the shortening of the days or the crisp nights. I just like to light fires. I use random things from the house as fuel. After the fire has really had a chance to get going, I extinguish the flames with water so that a mixture of steam and smoke rise. I inhale the smoke and steam and pretend I've torched someone's house and am now standing with everyone else watching the firemen get the blaze under control. Sometimes it's my house I am torching, sometimes it belongs to someone I know, sometimes it's a stranger's. Like a lot of sociopaths, I kill animals. I look in people's windows. I steal their mail. Just something to do. That is why I light fires. And since this is the end of things as they have been. I am moving behind the tree line and will be fading from the world as most know it to be. I think it's time to say goodbye to some things. It's time to terminate things. It's time to maim things so they remain alive long enough to get finished off by predators at dusk. It's time to close accounts, let the end be the end and be done.

I have been dragging my past with me like it's a dying comrade and we're trying to make it back to the beach after a mission gone terribly wrong. That was my youth. Like the Bay of Pigs. A piece of shit mission. Everyone knew it when they went out on that one and I knew it when I went out on mine. A bad mission. Old maps, faulty intelligence, no clear objective. Years after it was over, I blamed others for what it wasn't and what it could have been. At the time, I didn't think to blame anyone. One of the blindsides of youth is that you don't value that which is in great abundance and can't imagine things being any other way. You're only aware of what was, rarely of what is. It's a waste of time to blame others for anything. I should have seen it coming or dealt with it properly the first time. It's why some people kill their parents. Your father fucked you up? Is he still alive? Why don't you break his neck? You could stab him so many times you'd pass out from exhaustion over his dead body and slip in his blood when you finally left the scene. You could exterminate him from your thoughts, he's as good as dead and you don't do time. I had to do this with memories of my youth at a time when most of my life was ahead of me and not behind me as it is now. I had to hack its fingers off, it held on hard. Now that's all over with. A lot of things are over with. One could say that when something comes to an end, it's only because something else is beginning. That may be true, if you play with crystals and worship the moon. For me, it's always been about the mission and when it's over, it's death until the next one starts. I don't need love. I don't need friends. I need the next thing. I need the next reason to keep living. For a long time now, I have been in maintenance mode. I feed it and keep it in shape so it can deliver as well as expected with the accumulated wear and tear now being a performance factor. Every day, I get rid of something. Every day, I terminate a memory. Every day, I throw something out. The less I have, the less has me. The mission was bitched from the start. That's why I took it. It's why bad-end missions get taken all the time. The last thing you want to do is come back. The last thing you can do is come back. You can come back and live in the lie you have created for yourself, the lie that immediately surrounds you upon mission's end. I lived it for some time. Damn near killed me. I acknowledge zero community, zero peer group. A lot of people I knew have died. Some had it coming, some were old, some had bad luck. When some of them went, it hurt. It hurt badly and long. I realized that the hurt was from holding on, from straddling past and present and feeling the psyche tear. I've heard people say that pain and sadness are part of life and it's cowardly not to face them. I think that's an idea for idiots. Do you hold onto a hot coal? Drop it and move up the trail. I let the memories die. They are plants I don't water. They are chained up dogs that don't get fed. If I didn't do this, I would have killed myself years ago. I can't think of one single thing to live for but as long as I'm here, I might as well keep moving. The mission takes my mind off the fact that life is meaningless. When I am not out on it, I am here, throwing things away, seeing how much less I can live with, waiting for the next distraction. Youth and self-importance are gone. Need for human contact is almost gone. Now and again there's something, an echo of past need, an old weakness. I just let it starve to death. I threw out my walkie-talkie today. There's no one to walkie with and nothing to talkie about, is there? How are you? How are you getting along? Feeling alright? Fuck you. People ask these questions because either their lives are so inconsequential to them that small talk saves them from the pain of having to know something new or because they don't have the guts to exist without comparative analysis masked in time wasting verbal exchange. You always go to someone else for self-help. You need company for self-abuse. How am I? Here until I'm dead. How much pain am I in? As much as I let you put me in. Kindred spirit? No such thing. Good to go? Gone.

Sometimes it's hard not to hate you for your bovine, slow-eyed acceptance of servitude. Something's wrong alright. It's you. Like the dullards before you, there will be no spark of awareness and therefore no cowardice. Just the time, the payout, the slow bleed. The safety in huddled, stupefied numbers. You are owned and it makes you feel safe. You have always been on time that was loaned to you at steep interest rate. When they come to take you out, you never ask why. You will pay. Can you imagine what it's like for the poor, who work too hard for far too little? Who have known hardships you could never fathom? Who know pain as well as you can spell your name? Can you calculate how long and how silently they have suffered at your hands? Can you find the number of people you have sacrificed, whose lives you have destroyed, whose families you have shattered beyond repair? Do you understand what that means? They never get over it. They never get better. Every day, their lives are awful and they know exactly where to lay the blame but somehow, they will always blame themselves. Do you know what parents consider themselves when they bury their sons? Failures. Will you admit that you never knew what you were doing and you were never ready to give what you made others give? That you are and always will be a coward? A weakling preaching strength, who sends in the best to do the worst. You said you were going to lead them and let the chips fall where they may but you already knew where the chips were going to fall. You lied. You didn't lead. You're not a leader, you never were a leader and you will never be a leader. You gave orders. You ordered them into blind runs, into horror, disfigurement and death. They believed in the promise and the reward that you knew they would never receive. They paid. And now it's time for you to pay. Now it's time to send your children into the heat and the horror and the fury. No doubt your god will protect them. No doubt they will go, for they too believe in the promise you deliver in your hesitant, faltering speak. The words of an idiot who leads the deserving into the undeserved. And for this you will pay. Horror will visit you for the rest of your life because you have blood on your hands. Every life you have destroyed, every family you have torn apart, for all you have ruined in your stupidity and ignorance, you will pay. Yours is a study in underestimation. You underestimated the strength of those you purportedly serve. You thought they were all like you: intellectually lazy and easy to manipulate. You tried and quickly found that there were millions who see you for what you are and came back at you with righteous rage and hatred. Your cronies, who tried to wave us away with manipulated statistics and outright lies, underestimated the unrelenting tenacity with which we held onto the truth and the power of good. You and your sycophants could scarcely believe how much truth and freedom means to us because you think everyone is like you: compromised and without honor. You underestimated our belief in justice and how far we'll go to get it and what we're ready to part with to make sure you are stopped. And for this you will pay. And when the hyenas rip you to shreds and break your bones in their teeth, they will be consuming a coward and they will not care.

You are my inspiration. Your lies, your weakness, your toxic consumption, cowardice and ignorance have driven me to heights I thought unreachable. Because of you, I found myself. For years, for decades, I was the waiter with an assassin's dreams. I was the prisoner always carrying the handful of mortar from my cell to the yard. I was the one who worked hard and seemed the most dedicated when actually I was your greatest enemy. I smiled at your dinners and laughed at your jokes but in my mind I spat in your food and hoped for miscarriages. There wasn't one day that went by where I didn't know I was going over that wall to freedom. It will be my ultimate triumph. Even greater than not having children and stopping the hideous bloodlines of my parents. More triumphant than never succumbing to your tobacco, alcohol and obesity. More than never getting caught up in your knee high expectation and appalling lack of discipline, decency and delivery. There will be none of your noise, none of your neurotic mediocrity and denial. Your ghettos and picked scabs, the sewage you call culture and the cowardice that passes for your government will not compromise me as it has so obviously compromised you. I am leaving you to this oblivion. Hold on tight to the whirling, shrapnel spewing dragon that you allowed to decimate your population and rape the will of your young. They got you, they'll get your children. You are what you have been bred to be: The Atrocity. You can deny it but it's too late. You can hate me but it's no use. You can try to weaken and stop me but you will be unable. Your land has been overrun. Your cities have been turned into experiments in futility and banal violence marathons. My victory will be shown to none and known only by me. My perfect and complete win will take place in relative solitude, in clean sanity, clarity and strength. I am leaving. I am leaving and there will be no more. I will leave no forwarding address and my whereabouts and activities will be known only by accountants and lawyers. I will buy provisions with cash, never giving my name, making eye contact or uttering a word during transaction. There will be no conversations to have, no funerals to go to, no arguments or discussion. No betrayal or deceit. No dreams of vengeance or accumulated bitterness ready to erupt, no counting of days, no anticipation of rejection. What, you say? How can one go without these things? Why, they are the very stuff of life! Yes they are. They are if you're an idiot who waits for others to dictate how your life will play out. It's yours, right now. You and I have nothing to discuss. Your life and what you have achieved mean nothing to me. Your good deeds are meaningless in the world. History is silent. The present is a repeat of the mistakes of those who blundered before. There's no evolution, no progress to be had, no great discoveries to be made. The only relevant facts accrued in the past several decades helped to comprise an increasingly clearer picture of how the planet is being destroyed and how humans are toxic and disease ridden weak life forms. The miracle of human life is waiting to be revealed in answers to these questions: how did these pathetic, watery, weak, easily killed and utterly horrible animals last so long? How ultimately funny and terribly sad is it that their greatest achievements were their undoing? Denial, fear, greed and god. What an epitaph. The Atrocity. For me, a small living space, some good books and the rest of my life without you. After that, a death on my terms, body never found, personal possessions destroyed. Papers, photographs and all other documentation burned ahead of time. Complete and total victory over the wretched, merciless master who enslaves you. No me. Not ever.

Is there anything here I can call my own? A feeling? A moment? Anything? Will there ever be a time when I am truly loved? When I'll know it and not wonder if it's real? Is there something I can protect and love and care about? Is there a truth I can keep that has no fear attached? Will there ever be a time when I can be somewhere and it will feel like home? Will there ever be a time when I will look around me and know I am finally in the place I am supposed to be? Is there anything here, anything I can see, while I breathe and breathe, trying to stay alive long enough to just be able to be here and know that I am here? Not just any here but the here I am supposed to be in. Is there anything that I can call mine that will not eventually be taken from me? Is there anything, anyone, ever? We're sick and our bodies are breaking down. We're getting a lot of stuff cut off. Seems like we're under the knife more and more these days. We're getting melanomas cut out, lines filled in and scars removed from all the Botulinum Toxin shots we've been self-injecting for years. Sometimes I do up my girl and she does me or when we're fighting, we do ourselves. If you buy the street stuff it leaves deposits in the skin and sometimes you have to get that stuff cut out too. We're always getting something done. We look hot in magazines because they erase a lot of flaws and scars but really, we're scary up close and that's why we don't get too close to anyone but the help and our agents. My girlfriend and I live in a gated community. If we ever get lost, we can always buy one of those star maps to find our way home. We've never met any of our neighbors but I know they're hot. We're all hot, it's the only way you can buy a house in this neighborhood. It's gated. Cleaner than most but it's still pretty bad and you have to be careful. Last year we had rats all over the place outside near the garbage and under the porch. My acting-life coach-guru took tap water and put it into bowls and left it near the garbage cans and the rats drank it and in about a week we stopped seeing them alive. Saw a few dead ones. I haven't used water from the tap in years. Used to be you could bathe in it alright and not get any after effects but then a few years ago, people started getting red skin and scalp problems from it. So now we use bottled water and wash a lot less. We don't talk to each other as much as we used to. Our analysts told us that we are so self-involved now that we can only bear to process our feelings to ourselves. Our analysts also told us that the idea of dealing with someone else as they truly are is a concept that is completely foreign to us. They say it happens all the time but they also said chances are our relationship will be ok because even though we are unable to accept anyone but ourselves we are able to project ourselves on the other one so it's like being alone but with company. I guess that's why my girl and I get along. We're really not all that close but we're into the idea of people being close. Whatever. I try not to think about it too deeply. I try not to get too deep about anything. Why bother? Introspection is such a drag. I'd rather be able to fit into the same jeans for another decade and keep the lines in my face to a minimum. I leave the details to my manager. Details are not hot. I haven't talked to him for two years but there will be work at some point, for sure. We don't look like we used to. Our friends starting looking weird a few years ago and then we all kind of started looking the same, you know, big head, stretched face, frozen forehead, skinny body. I'm glad I'm not as hungry as I used to be. I want other people to have the food that I don't eat. Aren't there people in Africa who need it? Send it there. I am concerned about poor people and want everyone to have enough to eat. I think watching people eat is depressing. It's a sign you're poor or unhappy. Things are good. My blood is pretty clean and my abs are slammin'. My girlfriend's hot. We are hot. We are a hot couple. We have to be hot. It's good to be hot. My girlfriend's hot but she's not a hottie. It's not that she's too old—she's only 25 so she's got at least one good year left before she has to get the major overhaul. She's just a little overweight and a little behind on some SP's (surgical procedures). She'll be a semi-hottie or even a super-semi-hottie next summer for sure if she puts in the tanning bed time. She'll be hot but she'll have to tan up a lot to cover the scars from the SP's. We are ugly up close. We are scarred and tinted. Our hair is synthetic and stitched into our scalps. Our teeth rotted away years ago and we have fake ones drilled into our skulls. We don't touch. We are always healing from an SP and don't want to tear the stitching open or a cheek implant to get dislodged. We fear our security guards. They have guns and don't make much money. We have no guns and make a lot of money. They want what we have. We are hot. We are happening. We don't think because we let the thinkers do the thinking. It gives us more time to be hot. One of my manager's friends says I'm shallow. He's just jealous because he's always hungry and running late for something he has to be on time for. He thinks too much. He's not hot. No one pays him to be hot, he gets paid to be on time. I show up late and I'm still hot. My analyst says there's nothing he can do for me anymore because there's nothing more about me to analyze but he wants me to keep coming because when I am on his couch I look hot on it and make the room look hot and I like that. I like that a lot. Of course I'll keep going. I cough up blood but not in front of anyone but when I do it, I look hot.

I guess you really never stop loving someone. Even after the break up or the uprising, there is still the love. Actually, that's bullshit. I hate ones I used to love. I hate them for taking my vulnerability and smashing it to pieces and filling me with humiliation, confusion and shame. I don't spend a great deal of time thinking about them, but yes, I hate them. Hate is good. Hate is strong. Hate takes passion. Hate is not empty. Hate is not the end. Hate keeps the mind focused and the blood thin. There is still time for love even on a budget. A day in Hollywood is like a day anywhere else where they're slaughtering people at the workplace. Recently I made my affections known to a woman in Hollywood. I had been living in a box underneath an overpass downtown having just previously moved from a box located over an underpass but I kept getting run over by cars and killed and while being dead was not so bad and really cheap, I opted for the underpass location, life and less traffic. **Some people fear hate because they know it's**

real commitment and since they have cheated out on love as many times as they've walked through a door—they know that hate is different. They know that hate is for real and once it's there—it's forever. You can forgive someone but that's just for church or contractual obligations. You've got to stand up for your hatred. When you say you hate someone—that's when people start listening. Anyway, I turned in a friend's parents for reading books and was given a large sum of money by the state and moved into a house. I sent a message of love and a few hundred thousand dollars to a beautiful woman who lived down the street and asked if she would move in with me. She sent one of her servants over with a letter informing me that my love was not worth anything to her but she appreciated what I said because it made her feel hot and said I could have one of her legs, the left one from the knee down. Actually not her leg but the leg of one of her slaves. She sent the slave over with her husband. He hacked her leg off, left it on the front porch, cleaned my pool and the two of them left, he carrying her in his arms. Do you have the strength to hate? Maybe, maybe not. This is why hate gets a bad rap. Those who say it's bad are the ones who aren't strong enough to carry the weight of hate. In their minds, they wish they could hate out loud. They secretly hate but what good is that? It's not real hate. It's just cowardice. There it is: Concealed hatred is cowardice. I loved the leg immediately. I knew I had little time. I was losing her quickly. She was being wooed by many flies and even more maggots. A few short summer weeks later, I was left with some bones and nothing more. I made the bones into bone meal and had some bone meals and then one morning as I put my spoon down into the empty bowl, I realized that she was gone. Yes, she was gone but the love stays on. Perhaps there's hope for me.

Humans are lame. We are lame. I am lame. I am wretched, dull, self-absorbed, shallow, depressed, mean, cowardly, stingy and worse. I don't take part in life because it repels, disgusts and alienates me. With every breath, I maintain the flow of oxygenated blood to my brain so I can keep existing. I poison myself with life. The more time passes, the worse it gets. **That's why people get old, start malfunctioning, shrivel up and die—life catches up with them, finally overpowers them, poisons them and breaks their will so completely and with such overwhelming force they succumb to life and it kills them.** Do you know why not many people are born in Los Angeles? Most of the pregnancies that aren't aborted usually come out dead. Poisoned. Myself and my friends, we live behind a gate. We live in a community surrounded by an electrified fence. We get paid a lot of money. We never count it, we just have it. Just having it gets us everything for free. People like to give rich people things for free. It makes them feel they too are part of the dream. I don't know what money buys. I don't buy things, I am given things. I sometimes give money to the people I see scuttling around the compound. They look down and bow and mutter things I can't make out. I see them wash the money in the sink. They do that because it is said our touch poisons the money and they can get diseased from it. They wear rubber gloves when they take the money from my hand. When we fuck by the pool we bleed out of our mouths and can't finish. We are too toxic. Insects die when they touch us. We don't eat. We just talk to our people and take meetings with people hired to take meetings with us. Sometimes we leave the compound and go down into the city where people gasp and wave when they see us. We wave weakly back at them. We feel so sick. How do poor people get the energy to walk around? Have you ever seen them waiting for the bus, talking amongst each other, waving their hands and carrying on? So much animation. They seem happy. I can't understand what they have to be happy about though. They're not rich, they're not good looking, they're so common. Where do they live? Maybe in those disgusting houses I see on the way to the airport? Believe it or not, I have actually met some of these people. When we do crowd scenes in a film, we sometimes say hello to the extras from a safe distance. Sometimes they want to shake our hands and we send assistants out to do it because we really can't, you know, can't touch them. They understand. They're always so polite!

I am sick. Sick of people I know dying. I am sick of being left here when I am already here. I am sick of being left stranded when I am already stranded. I don't want to go with them but I am sick of their departure. I don't care what I sound like. I don't care that I sound pathetic or weak. I am neither. I am just sick of grief's weight. I see that I am strong when I am alone. Unwitnessed grief. I know it well. There is nothing like crying alone in a room. Nothing. I don't know how I do it exactly but I always end up with women who have sustained injuries to their heads. I meet a woman and we start going out and soon enough she tells me about the time she hit her head. Some were in car accidents, some fell, others walked into something that wasn't soft. It got to the point where if one of them didn't tell me about it, I would ask. They would ask me how I knew and wonder if they had done something that let me know. I told them no, I was just guessing. If one of them wouldn't show up to my small, low ceilinged room (the one with no moving air that smelled of sweat and dirty clothes), I just figured she hit her head and got lost or knocked herself out. But she would eventually show up, sometimes days late and it was always worth the wait. One woman showed me an amazing scar going along the back of her head and the places where the hair extensions had been attached. One had two false teeth. One had tripped and fallen twice, both times breaking her nose. None of these women were dumb, they were just unlucky and a little nuts I guess. I didn't mind, they spent nights with me and that was alright. Some of these women were pretty mean but never to me. I don't know why but they had a soft spot for me. One told me about all the guys she had spent time with just so they would buy her drugs. One had her friend drive her around town while she serviced men in the back of the car, the car was always on the move and thanks to a cell phone, she kept busy and made a fair bit of money. I was always appreciative of the things she bought me, especially seeing how she earned her income. I have to say, at this point, I think I prefer women who have sustained low to medium level blunt force trauma injuries to their skulls. They are more interesting and the sex is really good. There's something in their eyes, a certain disconnect that makes them exciting. I have been with well adjusted women who have never been bopped on the head and liked them but it would have been better if they had been cracked upside the cranium because while they were really cool they lacked that magical, whacked out rationale that in my experience, only seems to be the result of a cranial injury. One woman I went out with for awhile a couple of years ago was in a car accident and hit her head so hard, one of her eyes wouldn't move and she had this fixed half stare all the time. Sex was interesting with her. She always looked happy but distracted. She had crooked implants that kind of matched her smile and she was really cool. A nurse. Years ago I was going out with a woman and I was away for some weeks and called her from the road. She laughed while she told me that she had hit her head and gotten a few stitches. I laughed with her, it was funny. It's always funny. I torched two parked cars tonight. I feel great.

Came home and shot his wife and two small children. Sat on the back porch with a beer. Heard the sirens and put one through the roof of his mouth. What he couldn't control, he killed. I am old and can look back on many years. It took me a long time to understand but now I do. I used to wonder, what's the purpose of a life? I see now that life has purpose and meaning. The meaning of our lives, the reason we were put here, was to work and serve Him. Not to sing or to dance or to ask questions but to serve and work and be grateful for the chance to sacrifice. What better thing to do with a life?

Please Him, yes, please and serve. That was all there was to our lives and looking back, even though many of us were malnourished and died young, died forgotten in filthy ghettos, ruined and covered with lice, we felt somehow safe in His invisible but ever present embrace. We had nothing. But in that nothing, we had nothing to worry about, nothing to hope for and nothing to fear. Even though we never saw Him, never got to kiss His sleeve or wipe the dust from His boots, we all felt we knew Him, not in a intimate or unclean way, please tell me you understand, thank you.

When He sent our sons off to foreign lands to fight the enemies of the People, we felt blessed the blood of our blood had amounted to something. They left our village to directly serve Him. Believe me, we looked at our sons for what we knew would be the last time and I have to say, some of us, even though we had spent our lives working from dawn to dark, felt that we were lesser men for not having the strength to go with these younger men, these fortunate warriors of the nation. We were so proud to see them in their uniforms. We held back tears as they waved goodbye.

All this was many years ago. The wars are over now, so we are told. None of our sons came home and no one ever came to tell us what happened to them. Our daughters left for cities and never returned. Life went on. Now many of us are dying or dead. There are only a few of us left in the village and no children live here. We live close to each other and wait for the days to end. Many of us are too weak to work the fields so we can only grow a little. The winters are hard on us. It has been a life as good as any other.

I will admit this to you as long as you promise not to tell anyone. I do admit a sadness. I miss my children so. I don't care that I have been hungry all my life. I don't mind that I have worked hard since I was a child and it's all I know. I am sad sometimes in the winter evenings when the sun is disappearing below the land. I am sad that life is coming to an end and that I have never been anywhere and that I never had a chance to see Him. The Great One, the Father of all lands. The Father of all who live in this great nation. If only for a moment, if only to fall at His feet and beg forgiveness for not being able to give Him more than two sons and all my wheat. Please understand, it was all I had. I know that it was not enough and it fills me with sadness when all is dark and cold and quiet.

Please forgive me, no one should talk like this, with these small and worthless words. One should only see the truth—that all things happen for a reason and everything is a blessing. When one starves, it's for a greater good and the one who is hungry should cling to life with every breath but most of all, be grateful, grateful to be alive to serve Him. When one toils ceaselessly, is it not a blessed event? To have a body to serve with, is that not all the blessing one could hope for?

Every morning when the sun comes up over the land, we get on our sore and sorry knees, our bones stiff from work and age creak as we kneel down upon the merciful earth that has given us so much, more than we could ever give back to it. To this land, we can only repay with our worthless, wretched bodies. We get on our filthy knees and turn our knotted, crooked hands to the sky and thank Him for all He has given us. That we lived longer than He did is to our greatest regret. How dare we be blessed with another day while His eternal rest is no doubt interrupted constantly by our pitiful wails as we mourn His passing? How dare we speak? How dare we do anything else than work and collapse and rise to work again? How dare we feel anything but shame at our slothfulness and fervent gratitude for all His blessings? I have never dared to ask many questions besides these.

But yes, many nights, we waited. We waited for our sons to come back to us. We waited for His arrival. We waited. We cleared the large room in our small home and kept it clean and unoccupied in case He came to us and needed shelter and rest. On these endless nights of waiting, one family member sat awake and vigilant to open the door for Him and welcome Him into our miserable home. On the winter nights I was posted, I sat up with my teeth chattering, scratching at the hungry bite of lice, almost lightheaded with anticipation as my eyes ceaselessly scanned the darkness, I felt nothing but gratitude. Nothing more, sir. Nothing. The only questions I would dare to ask, sir, are these: Did I give enough? Could I have given more? I must admit, sir, these questions have kept me from sleeping many nights.

Come on little tadpole, don't be afraid. Time to evolve. Crawl towards the shallows where the slime turns orange. That's acid residue. This is the LA

River, the place you've been living for the last 41 days. Your mother left you here because she didn't want you. Crawl up the embankment to the highway. Open your little eyes. Do you know what that is in front of you? That's a police officer. He will hurt you. Do you feel that tingling in your spine? That's your first twinge of paranoia. Hold onto this moment! This is the purest feeling you will ever have. You will spend the rest of your life trying to feel as alive as you do right now! You will make enough money to buy consumer poison and live in a small room and grind your life into powder. You'll fuck women with missing teeth and running sores. You'll buy drugs from their boyfriends and listen to compact discs of their bands. You're in LA now, your life is already over. Come on little tadpole, you mongoloid rapist. Time to go. Tourist information. When you enter Los Angeles, the best thing to do is immediately take cover. Dive for it! Stay low! There's less chance of a head shot if you stay down. If you take a shot to the head, no ambulance will come. You're going to bleed out and they won't be able to do anything for you. The hospitals are already filled with less life threatening examples of injury: a short blade stabbing, low caliber bullet in the jaw, knife stuck in a leg—your typical Saturday night stuff. For a low price, you can fix yourself! They give you the anatomy and basic ER procedure books and there's even a floater who goes from table to table to watch over and advise (but cannot in any way be held liable for information, advice or action that leads to the death of a patient or amputation of a limb or any result that could in any way be termed "negative." These are non-negotiable points and immediately go into effect as soon as anyone walks through the doorway of the DIY ward. So don't even think of trying to bring your "case" to one of those Judge Judy pieces of shit or we'll beat and rape you until you beg to be killed to stop the pain). Kind of like tech support. You pay for the disposable instruments, morphine and plastic sheets. I know what you're thinking. No. You can't stab yourself in the leg, limp in and buy morphine cheap. It's really expensive and they only sell small quantities so don't even think about it. If you sign the waiver, you can bring your own stuff though.

In some places, like the Rampart Division, they don't even have the waiver, you can do what you want. Some of these gangster guys have become surprisingly efficient at slug extraction, closing punctures and even sterilizing wounds. That's what usually gets people, the infection a few days later. Wounds swell and tear open, abscesses, lesions, gangrene, septic infection. Good thing for that waiver or the courts would be tied up even worse than they are now! Anyway, just stay the hell down and there's a good chance you can avoid an unfortunate experience like this! If you are moving to or even just visiting the city of Los Angeles (the name by the way, roughly translates into "The land of many ruined fuckers," or more concisely, "The crippled ones"), you will have a lot of things to get used to. First off, the air. You will spend a good period of time in different levels of distress as your lungs and heart acclimate to the quality of air. Symptoms include vomiting, seizures, thickening of the blood, insomnia, ringing in the ears, diarrhea, blindness, erratic heart beat, hair loss and impotence. Others may experience depression, listlessness and an overwhelming sense of hopelessness. Visitors don't worry! Many of the better hotels feature oxygen tanks in lightweight back packs or on wheelies with affordable day rates and some of the four star hotels have entire floors with relatively clean and breathable air and executive suites providing bulletproof windows and panic rooms. These rooms are not cheap and go fast around holidays and premiers so go online and get your reservations ASAP! Those of you planning to spend a longer period of time in "The Filthy Cripple" are advised to just dive in and get it over with. It's like getting jumped into a gang or raped in prison—hurts at first but then you're in. (When you stop seeing blood in your urine, you've adjusted. Welcome!) Ok, so we've covered the air, what's next? Next on the list would be dealing with the law enforcement community. You will have interactions with police, there's no question about that. How bad you're going to get it is totally up to you and lady luck. If you're white, you can expect the routine body search, car search and occasional kidney punch while cuffed. If you're white and you see a police officer within a city block of you and he or she (it's hard to tell them apart with the growth hormone injections they're required to take these days) starts walking towards you, the best thing to do is avoid eye contact and do not, and I cannot overemphasize this, do not speak to a Filthy Cripple law enforcement officer unless they speak to you. I have seen senior citizens thrown to the ground, pepper sprayed and cuffed for asking directions to Mann's Chinese Theater, their oxygen tanks getting hopelessly scratched and dented in the process. Eye contact and verbal communication that is not initiated by the law enforcement official is regarded as confrontational and threatening. They are within the law to take you down. So, what do we do when we see FCPD officers? That's right, we walk slowly, hands in plain sight, back into where we came out of. Some visitors never get out of the lobby of the hotel. Be prepared to spend extra days to see the sights. Preparation is key. For those of you who are not white, here are some tips to avoid getting maimed, killed or otherwise detained by the men and women of the FCPD: there are skin lightening and eye rounding treatments available. Look at what Michael Jackson was able to achieve in just several long, expensive and painful visits to the dermatologist! They couldn't get to the skin underneath his nails, hence the band-aids he wears on his fingertips in public, although some close to him will tell you that he sometimes puts on the bandages to avoid getting the fecal matter of children in his cuticles. Also, non-whites are advised to do anything they can to "seem" Caucasian or otherwise unthreatening. The music of Loggins & Messina, Beck or Sean Combs playing in your rental car when driving can make police hesitate to pull you over and smash your head in. A cup of Starbucks coffee in plain sight is a good thing too. Let's get onto the fun stuff. The Big Filthy is a colorful and relentlessly fascinating place to furtively lurk and fearfully view others. Seeing some of the locals will give you stories to keep your friends and relatives nauseated and glued to their chairs for hours when you get back to America. Here's a few things to expect (notebooks out shutterbugs!): You can expect to see a lot of people who appear to have wire protruding from parts of their skulls or faces. These are genuine abortion survivors and make up over 28% of our population! Many of you remember the report Geraldo Rivera (real name Jerry Rivers) filed on these brave and tortured souls only to reveal at the end of the hour that he too was an abortion survivor and proudly showed the scar where the coat hanger had been removed years ago. Well, not everyone can afford this surgery, so now and again you will see these people who were meant to be dead. Feel free to make donations to them but don't take the prayer card they give in return because they are usually infected with something untreatable. Before we go further, a note to parents: Do not let your children feed the homeless when they come up to the windows of the tour bus. Children and others have lost fingers and suffered painful injuries this way. These people are hungry! We in the city of dried blood and bullet casings have a thing about always looking our best so expect to see a lot of surgical enhancement! Huge breasted and fish-lipped men (and women) are common on these garbage strewn and vomit splattered streets. They are usually up for a photo op and if you're lucky, you can see them drain the putrid, black fluid from the sores on their legs! But most of the time, they're on their way to an audition and only have time to perform brief sex acts at surprisingly affordable prices. To make the entertainment industry work, it's go go go! Many tours of the star's homes are available and can be booked with the hotel concierge. Due to the recent rash of tourist deaths stemming from over-zealous security, many star's homes are now off-limits. Sharon Stoned's bungalow is a no-go for tourists now due to the three deaths that occurred near her property last month. She was quoted in the monthly magazine White Right as saying, "There's a sign in front of my home that says, 'MY DOGS EAT KIDS.' People must think I'm joking. Wanna see my snatch? It'll cost ya." Although Ms. Stoned's acting career is flat line, and one of the Disney head honchos recently referred to her as, "That psycho cunt," she is MENSA and never jokes. She also eats Spam brand potted meat product and has on occasion, vomited large quantities of human and canine fetal remains while walking down the red carpet of movie premiers. She rubs the chunks into the carpet with her shoes and pretends no one notices. Hey, Hugh Grant hired a whore to service him on Sunset Blvd., got busted and no one noticed besides Jay Leno. People are still sacrificing small animals at the spot where Hugh the Spew was apprehended. Guess we're noticing now. Thanks Jay! We have so many stars, directors, agents and other whores here, I could go on for days with their stories! Come visit, come see why people hate and fear LA, the glittering smile of the great Satan! On a side note, I just wanted to say that tampons are smaller these days because women are bleeding less. Know why? Because the human race is drying up. Soon all women will look like Calista Dogheart; breastless, terrified, neurotic. We wonder why Hollywood starlets adopt. We have theories. They adopted because:

a. They feel sorry for orphaned children.
b. They didn't want to interrupt their careers with pregnancy.
c. Their wombs are lined with alkaloid and sulfate deposits and nothing can grow there.
d. Other

I know this is off topic but I had to tell you this: I heard that the part of the Pentagon that was destroyed on September 11th 2001 was not, I repeat not, the part of the structure where the gas chambers are located. They are in a different part of the building and many floors below. This refutes the article in Strolling Stoned. The head editor of said publication does what a lot of people all over the world do all the time: he performs oral sex on young men with relish, gusto and gratitude. I say this to dispel rumors that this activity only takes place in back rooms of the Vatican and other Catholic venues. I'm saying it's ok. I'm saying it's ok to come home. I'm saying everything's going to be alright. Enjoy your stay!

My scar tissue tells my tale. My name is not important. Only the truth I tell and the journey I have made are of any worth. The rest is just the

sound of wind and boots stepping down endless trails of cinder littered with bones and scraps of metal. You asked of us and so we gave. We gave you our arms and legs. We gave you our eyes and teeth. You said we were in danger and there was no choice but to fight. We could not see this enemy but you said they were at our door and so we followed you. We obeyed you. You were our leader. But then things changed. Slowly at first, we noticed that what you said wasn't exactly the truth but we figured we were mistaken, surely there's more to truth than mere citizens can understand. Months turned into years and almost at once, we were no longer able to live without our arms and legs and eyes and teeth, these things that you have that many of us no longer have. We grew angry when it finally dawned on us that the great sacrifice we made with honor and dignity before our friends, families and the entire world was nothing more than a mere whim on your part. That so many brave were lead to death and mutilation by such a fool is heartbreaking but to ultimately find that we were lured away from our paths of virtue and honor into this distant kill zone by a coward, is inexcusable. Although you are not here to bear witness, history has judged you harshly and deservedly so. Had you taken the time to learn some history, you would know that all empires fall and all dynasties end. Your reign was neither. It was a just a series of business transactions and scandal at the ballot box. You were the investment and before you were executed, you paid off well. The surviving wealthy you enabled will sing your praises until the end but they do so from foreign shores as they either took advantage of the thirty day amnesty that allowed them to flee or face execution in the same manner you did. It is of great joy to some and slight regret to others that your wife and two daughters were beheaded along with you in that basement all those years ago. Most say death to the beast and the same unto the family of the beast. You should have learned your history. You should have understood the people who you were charged to protect and serve. We are, for the most part, a good and courageous people. As a nation, we have suffered much and given much to the world. Why you chose to betray us, is to many, a great mystery. What you were thinking and what lead you to make the choices you did are of little concern past tea house chatter at this point. That was the past and the future, God willing, is ever so bright. Unlike you, your successor, President Abu Musab al-Zarqawi is a true and honest leader, a great scholar, a warrior and not a coward. "Death to Cowards" was carved into your stomach. This is not legend. We all saw your head hanging from the fist of one of the guards. It was a great day of celebration when the bodies of you and your family were burned. On a personal note, I will miss the White House but the Mosque that has taken its place is breathtaking and enchants thousands of visitors every day. Many is the evening I have knelt in prayer on the grounds. La Allah illa Allah!

Memories of boys mugging the two boys. I still don't know how to handle even the most subtle hint of threat to my person. If someone was to say as little as, "You better hurry up," it's not even fighting words, it's a matter of surviving by smashing the skull of this person with the closest thing. It's not even a decision. It comes as quickly and unconsciously as dropping something hot. Even a comment in a letter, someone takes issue with something I am doing, if it feels threatening, and most of the time it does, I want to hack the man's ear off so he'll understand. I want him to understand I'm sensitive and fragile. That I have had a traumatic past and am easily frightened. I also want him to know that if I could, I would tie him to a chair and make him watch me hack his girlfriend to pieces. My father liked the leash. He did well with it around his neck and he enjoyed putting it around the necks of his many dogs. He was used to ownership, that is to say, he was used to being owned. He was a company man. He worshipped order and extracted large amounts of comfort from serving his superiors. Since he had no leadership qualities of his own that he could successfully exert over any human besides receptionists and hotel personnel, he derived great pleasure from pulling sharply upwards on a short piece of leather attached to a choke chain around a dog's warm throat. He would pull with great force, he drew his strength from cold humiliation filled nights of his wife's dry refusal, her scaly hand slapping at his tentative exploration of her abandoned sex. He drew his strength from rage at yet another failed marriage he was determined to stick out because he was too old to start over and completely incapable of aping humanesque qualities to lure a woman of any substance into his life once more. He drew the strength of a loser, a strength that only surfaces to viciously attack when advantage is imagined. With this cold strength and teeth clenched hard, he pulled the short leash. The chain bit into the dog's neck as the front feet left the ground. The animal, and I say animal, because when you do this to any creature, people included, they default to the lowest and most urgent survival mode. The eyes of the animal would go wide and a choked breath would escape though the chained windpipe. The paws would come back to the ground and the animal would cough, seemingly trying to dislodge something from its throat. The animal's tongue would come out farther than it ever did any other time and the animal seemed on the verge of vomiting. Then he would say the word that justified the act. "Heel." On several occasions, I saw some of the dogs shake and urinate freely while they sat with their teeth chattering in front of him, his right index finger an inch over the animal's nose. He terrified them and they seemed dedicated to this fear. The dogs were bound to his cruelty. And for a time, so was I. I understand the captive who protects his captor. I understand the people who stay in abusive relationships and wear their bruises proudly. Sad, mean brutal cycle. After awhile, if you want it bad enough, if you really need it—anything will feel like love.

Happiness left me when I saw that things end. That your desire, passion and commitment don't mean much. You're just left to walk though the debris of your effort. What was a beautiful machine eventually turns into an ignored relic. But it's not a relic. I'm not. This is the flood season. **ONE** This is the draught. This the bleached field harvest. This is Amerika now. Amerika Now. Amerika as it's always been. From shackled, exhausted imports captured and sold into Amerikana, to laid back super-cooled star map execs sliding out of meetings, silk on leather and back into traffic. Amerika **NATION** is the equation that we waited centuries to see worked out over land and sea, in third world countries and postwar alliances. Millions of gallons of soft drink potion poured over a planet that screams and dies for clean water. Millions of tons of napalm dropped for hippie spit, the shame of a nation and post traumatic wife beatings. In the **IN** present day, millions are stricken with classic self-serve wonderment at why things are the way they are. So deep in fear, they look everywhere but to themselves. This is the landscape of fear. This is the land of the free and the home of the brave but no one remembers those **A** parts as well as they acknowledge fear and paranoia as normal operating procedure and bravery as the occupation of idiots who couldn't get a better paying job. The racism and seething hatred of the poor that is inherent in the very fiber of Amerikana is now the waste receptacle **RUT** that has been overfilled, compacted, overfilled again and now runneth over. They cannot build prisons fast enough for all the new entries into the criminal class. No religious tract will protect you against panic. The Christians are more afraid than ever. They are terrified and giddy with the thought that it can only get worse. Fear helps their work. Fear widens the orifice and lowers the level of resistance. *"Put your guns up boys, it's just some niggers. Goddam y'all nearly got your dumb black asses shot. We thought y'all were Jews."* Their waking state of fear sends their Zealot division to the streets to spread fear to others so they too can feel the fear and take part in the war against sanity. Pat Robertson of the Christian Coalition is getting it on and banging a gong.

"Just like what Nazi Germany did to the Jews, so liberal America is now doing to the evangelical Christians. It's no different. It is the same thing. It is happening all over again. It is the Democratic Congress, the liberal-based media and the homosexuals who want to destroy the Christians. Wholesale abuse and discrimination and the worst bigotry directed toward any group in America today. More terrible than anything suffered by any minority in history." —Pat Robertson, 1993 interview with Molly Ivins.

"I think we ought to close Halloween down. Do you want your children to dress up as witches? The Druids used to dress up like this when they were doing human sacrifices... [Your children] are acting out Satanic rituals and participating in it, and don't even realize it." — Pat Robertson, "The 700 Club," 10-29-82.

Pat Robertson's website suggests you do the following at Halloween:

01. Fill Baggies with candy and, include a fun, "child-friendly" tract in each bag, telling them about God's love. Once you've prepared these bags of goodies, it's important to ask God to bless the children who receive the packages.

02. Display the "House of Light" removable sticker. This will let others know that you are participating in the fun but not celebrating Halloween.

03. Wear a tee-shirt or sweatshirt with a Christ-centered message.

Unseen and unknown, the scabbed legions walk miles through solitary nights of hell, spewing blood-salt vomit and pieces of stomach lining. Feast or famine. Feat of feast: don't drink the good stuff if you know you're gonna hurl. Feat of famine: one more breath. Don't worry about the Christian Right taking over politics and dissolving the fine line between church and state. Worry about the Christian Right taking over McDonald's, thus erasing the line separating church and food that fattens you, clogs your arteries and otherwise fucks you up. Don't worry about the Christian Right putting prayer back in schools. Worry about putting students back in schools. It's the same sad old story, the one that made Amerika great. Poor dumb motherfuckers getting rawdealed by rich mean motherfuckers. And so it plays out. It's that whole overstuffed waste receptacle thing. Pray! Pray for: No more rape. No more child abduction. Pray Amerika doesn't get attacked again. Put your head down and pray. Pray before it's too late. If only all those people in the towers had believed in one god. If only we didn't live in a nation of Jews, Muslims, faggots and other heathens, everything would be fine, right? He's coming. He's coming. He's not breathing hard and faking it. He's really coming this time.

I have felt it in the past. Attraction to a woman. It always came with a certain measure of self-disgust. It happened recently. There I was with this woman. Not letting anything show. Not allowing one crippled display of vulnerability to register. Years ago, fear of rejection and eventual, long burning humiliation kept my feelings in check. Now it's different factors that keep my emotions stillborn. I have arrived at myself. I am beyond humiliation. Failure falls off me. Rejection is a given. The main thing that keeps me to myself is just knowing there's no way. There is just no way. At this point, what could my line possibly be? "Hi, I'm dead. Want to watch me sit silently in a small room? I can show you the parts of the ceiling my brains will most likely stick to." It is sad. To not need anyone. They ordered me out of the trench where I had been working for I don't know how long. I was standing on my own but when the guards grabbed the shoulders of my coat, I suddenly felt weak and my legs felt like they were made of wet rope. One of the guards told me to spell my name. I did. He motioned me to join a small group of men huddled a few feet away and told me to wait. I walked over and stood with them. We all looked alike. Grey skinned, scalp shaved down to stubble, starving to death. Our lives were not worth what little food we got. A guard once told me the lice that crawled all over our carcasses and fed on our blood were of more worth than we were. All of us in the group of freezing ghost men were Polish and I was sure that we were all going to be executed. It had happened before. A guard would come into the barracks and call out names and the men would scramble off the shelves we slept on and hurry themselves into their shoes but the guard would tell them not to bother, just to line up and get out of the barracks. The guard would look at the rest of us and say, "Back to sleep. Soon it will be your turn."

This day was different. Several minutes later the guard came back to where we stood and told us we were being released. All I could think of was my wife and son. I had thought of them every day all the years I had been here. I didn't know if they were alive or where they were but I thought of them as a prayer to keep breathing. I knew my parents were dead, my wife's too.

Months later, I was back in my village in Poland. I was told that my wife and son were taken away several days after I had been taken. No one knew where they were or if they were alive. I was told I had been gone over three years.

This was almost fifty years ago. I am happy to be alive. I live alone. I have lived alone since I was allowed to leave Kolyma. During all those years, there has been much loneliness and sadness in my thoughts, as if I were back in the mines. I wonder about my wife and child. Where are they? Are they alive? Do they wonder where I am? I ask God, why must there be this sadness, this cold darkness? What is this supposed to teach me? Are you trying to tell me something I cannot understand? But there is no answer, just silence.

The years and life have passed me. Sometimes I wake up in the middle of the night when the coldness of the air makes it impossible to sleep and for a moment I think I am back in Kolyma trying to sleep on a wooden plank with all the other men. We were barely able to keep ourselves fed but we kept the fleas and lice feasting to no end. When a man would die on the planks, one could see the parasites fleeing from his body. Some nights I find myself scratching when there is no itch.

In spite of all this sadness, in spite of what I have been through, being one of the "Men of Kolyma" (Kolyma, known as the "White Auschwitz," the coldest place in the world inhabited by man), I feel full of life and blessed. I am happy in spite of everything. Over three million men sent to Kolyma died of cold, starvation, exhaustion, execution or torture but for some reason I was spared. I see now that the camp was my life. Nothing up to that point mattered besides the lives of my wife and child but they are gone. I remember the camp more vividly than my wife's voice. I am grateful for every sunrise, every moment, every meal—everything. Bless all who walk upon this earth with kindness for his fellow man because it is only kindness and mercy that separates us from the absolute depths of hell.

You were the wolf who stood at the edge of my campfire every night. I would call to you but you would not come closer. A few nights later it was very cold and the fire was very bright and we could see each other's faces. You saw it in me and I saw it in you and you came and sat next to me and warmed yourself. We were together from then on and nothing could separate us. The world lost its hold on us. We won out against time and convention. I know I am rusted metal scraping against sidewalks of forgotten cities, an unheard groan of a freezing pipe in a condemned building. I know, I know. Believe me, I know. I know my words vaporize and lose all meaning as they evacuate my mouth. I know that all the years spent, all the miles traveled, all the sleep lost—just time wasted. Time wasted! Like leaving a lamp burning in an unoccupied room. A waste! What a horrible thing, time wasted. The ravages of futility. Inspiration's annihilating backhand. At the end of the trail, to find the pockets heavy with fool's gold, the ribs cracked from the last cheap shot and the heart helplessly empty . . . what a waste. And even though this is the cheaply woven fabric of my life, even though I am the hand that knocks unwelcome and uninvited on doors of empty houses, the cultivator of insufferable misery on hot endless nights of paranoia. Ceaselessly unendurable and obsessive repetition. A life nailed to the ground by dulled cowardice and uninventive thought. In spite of all that, there was a time when I . . . when I thought something more than all this was in my grasp. There was a time when I could feel the ground underneath my feet and I walked forward into time instead of standing still, stranded in semi-darkness with skewed memories of the past to keep me. I don't remember when I pulled back. I don't remember when I called it a day. I don't remember when I slipped underneath the surface of life and ended up here. I don't remember. I don't know.

Nothing can be recaptured. It can only be approximated and stood next to. It can only be lied into legend. Its corpse can only be mounted and displayed as a garish memento of what is lost. I want my MTV on PCP. I want to see tourists in Hollywood make a circle around Rosie O'Donnell. She's lying on her side. She's breathing heavy and slow. Labored. She's 713 pounds. Authorities took one of her children away. She ate the other two before they could get them away from her. She eats buckets of afterbirth contributed by Cedars-Sinai Hospital. She has two rows of leathery teats dotting her scarred stomach. Lice and other parasites run in the coarse hair that covers most of her body. The offspring of Scientologists punch and kick her midsection, positioning her for a meal. Scientologist goon security kick the homeless away from her and push their followers up to the front and down to the bloody teats. One man manages to break through security and bashes Rosie O'Donnell in the ribs with a length of pipe. Rosie O'Donnell's mouth opens and she convulsively regurgitates chunks of human fetal remains. An assistant with rubber gloves and knee-high rubber boots carefully guides the chunks back to Rosie O'Donnell's gaping mouth with a long-handled squeegee. Rosie O'Donnell's jaws work spasmodically up-taking the meal. An announcement is made through the small PA system telling the small crowd gathered that Rosie O'Donnell is fed several times a day. A press liaison to a group of V.I.P's from the EU tells the group that there are many unwanted children in the world and Rosie O'Donnell wants them. She wants them all.

I would give you the map to where all the landmines on my property are. I would part the razor wire so you could join me behind the tree line. I don't care if I ever see any of them again but I could look into your eyes for a long time. It's safe back here behind the tree line. Can you hear me calling to you from across the river? Please come. Hurry. There's not much time. The snipers will be back at their posts soon and crossing will be risky. Please hurry to my heart. I need to hear your breath explode against my neck. There is only this clenched moment. I would like to some day go home. I don't know the exact location of this place. I'm know I'm not there now. There would be a pleasing feeling of familiarity and a sense of welcome in everything I saw. People would greet me warmly. They would remind me of the length of my absence and the thousands of miles I had traveled in those restless years but mostly, they would tell me that I had been missed and that things were better now that I had returned. Autumn would come to this place of welcome, this place I would know to be home. Autumn would come and the air would grow cool, dry and magic. At night, I would walk the streets and not feel lonely or in need, for these were the streets of my hometown. These were the streets that I had thought about when far from them and now I was back and all was as it should be. The trees and the falling leaves would welcome me. I would look up at the moon and remember seeing it in countries all over the world as I had ceaselessly journeyed for decades, never remembering it looking the same as when viewed from my hometown.

Beat the history books until they stop lying. Know the tyranny of man and know all history. Crystallize your hatred. Strengthen it at every possible opportunity. Give it legs and eyes and purpose. All you need is the truth. Do not run from confrontation—it is the reward for all the hard work you have put in. Those who oppose you, they need not mercy or consideration. They were, at one time, given ample quantities of both and willingly squandered them. Your harshest actions against them are not only justified—they are absolutely necessary. Mussolini got what he deserved. Make no mistake about it. I want you to wake up in your bed next to something cold. I want you to turn on the light and see that you're lying next to the smoke charred, blasted apart body of a dead Marine. I want you to scream and jump out of the bed and try and leave the room only to find that the floor is slick with blood and littered with the limbs and torsos of American soldiers. I want you to be overwhelmed by the stench of burnt flesh, hair and blood. I want to you to slip and fall onto the floor and be covered by blood, ash and entrails. I want every meal you eat to contain the flesh of dead American soldiers. I want you to take the cover off the top of your breakfast tray, smell the cordite and see part of a human leg and some teeth. I want the lawn of the White House to be covered with the amputated limbs of the wounded housed at Walter Reed Army Hospital. I want you to see, smell and taste what you've done. I want to you roll around in it. I want you to watch a young soldier step on a landmine or walk by an I.E.D. as it detonates. You're a war time president and you need to know what these young men know. You should lose a finger for every thousand KIA and every thousand amputations. I think it's only fair. You're a war time president and I want you to be able to hold your hands up to the cameras of the world and say that the enemy fears freedom and that you are the commander and chief. You are the commander and chief, even though you don't lead the charge. Even though you have never been in a war. Even if you don't have the strength to carry out the orders you direct. You need to get some respect.

Most people share my opinion—that you're a coward and that you have a price to pay. I want all your suits to have blood splatter from American soldiers injured or killed in war. I want to see blood or body parts on the stage of every press conference you conduct and speech you make. You're anti-abortion because you don't believe in killing innocent life. You wait for them to grow up so they will know what they are risking. You wait for them to grow up because sales of all the food, clothing and tobacco needed to raise a child invigorates the economy, so they can't die too soon. You wait for them to become adults, innocence free and fair game. I want to lock you in rooms with grieving mothers and not allow you to leave for days at a time. I want them to be able to tell you everything about their dead sons. I want you to spend time with the wives of dead and mutilated young men and feel the grief and sorrow and living hell you have created for these people. I want you to bury all the dead. I want you, with a blood and guts stained suit, to put the shovel into the ground and dig a hole for the body. It's more worthwhile than anything you will ever do in office besides pay back what you have done by putting a gun in your mouth and exiting your brains all over the wall. After that momentous bit of domestic policy, we bring in your idiot brother and he cleans up the mess you made. He is then covered with American soldier blood, black and rancid from decomposition and he starts digging the holes, wearing the necklace of enemy ears, eating the rotting flesh of American war dead and stepping over piles of bodies and body parts that will be placed in his house and lawn. Your lovely daughters will be sent into the war as many lovely American daughters have before them. They will come back either in bags or on a stretcher. Your wife will smear their blood on her face every day. This is right. This is just. This is what we ask of you. If you do not give us what we deserve, we will give you what you deserve.

I loved you. I loved your mind and the way you thought. I loved being with you. I never thought I could care about someone as much as I cared about you, but I did. Do you know what you did to me? You put me in a jar and

screwed the lid on. Then the phone rang and you took the call. Then some friends came over. You swept the cans and bottles off the table after they left hours later. The jar with me inside went out with all the empties. You never once thought to look and see if I was ok. You killed me. I'm in a trashcan at the bottom of a wet paper bag with a bunch of empty beer bottles. I'm dead too, which sucks. How I met my girlfriend. I was in the aisle seat in the business class section of a flight from Denver to Dulles International in Washington DC. Across the aisle from me was a beautiful woman in a smart business suit. The flight attendant came up to her and asked if she would like some water or juice before we took off and she requested water. The sound of her voice sent me. Just her saying, "Oh, water, thank you," made me want to know her. I know that sounds stupid but I think you can tell a lot about someone by how they speak, how they phrase words and time their delivery. If you think about it, a lot of people don't speak distinctly, they just hurl words out of their mouths and make their point. Then there's some people who really know how to speak and it's fantastic to listen to them.

All of a sudden I heard that beautiful, sonorous voice speak again, and this time it was directed at me.

"Excuse me, I don't mean to pry but how did you come across Max Frisch?" she said as she tapped a long delicate index finger on the cover of the book I had on my tray table.

"You know Max Frisch?" I asked. I was amazed that she was talking to me and talking to me about Max Frisch.

"I can't believe you're reading Man In The Holocene, that's one of the most incredible short reads ever. I hope I'm not bothering you."

"No, not at all. Actually, a friend recommended one of his other books, I'm Not Stiller, which I read and loved and from there I went onto his book Homo Faber which . . ."

"Which got made into a movie that I saw on a plane and want to see again and can't find anywhere." She interjected.

"That's right, got made into a movie that I too saw on a flight and have been going to Amazon.com now and then for years trying to find a copy with no luck, and then onto Man In The Holocene which I have started twice and couldn't find for some time because it fell behind some other books on a shelf. I just found it and so I am starting again and hoping to get through it this time."

"It's such an amazing idea for a book." She said.

"I'm far enough into it now to see that it's going to be really great." I said.

"Are you a book fan? I hope I'm not bothering you but it's not often you see someone on a plane or anywhere else ever reading something that isn't off the rack."

"No, you're not bothering me at all, are you kidding?" I replied, "I was raised with books. My mother was an avid reader and we used read aloud to each other and all these years later, I am always looking for that amazing read. Of all the things I have ever experienced art, music, movies, paintings, photography, it's always books that have moved me the most. Most of my heroes are writers."

"If you could sit next to any writer alive or dead on a long flight, who would it be?" She asked.

"Can't I just sit with you?" I asked. I couldn't believe I said that but I did.

She laughed and said, "My name is Tania."

"Tania, I'm Karl."

"Is that with a C or with a K?" she asked.

"K. Is it Tan ya, or ia?"

"With an ia. Why?"

"This sounds like complete bull but it's true. Tania is my favorite name for a woman. I think it's from when I was young and Patty Hearst did that whole thing with the Symbionese Liberation Army and changed her name to

Tania. I just thought the name was cool. There's something about it, I don't know. In any case, that's the truth. It's nice to meet you." Rarely do you mean that. I truly did.

"It was Che Guevara's girlfriend's name and it's nice to meet you too, Karl with a K as in Karl Marx. Since you like books so much, have you ever tried writing any yourself or am I speaking to a published author whose books I promise to run out and buy at the earliest opportunity?"

"I have read enough great books to know for sure that I don't have anywhere near the talent to string together a novel. I admire those who can, though. I do have some good stories in me, just not the talent to put them across."

"What's the craziest story you have?" She asked.

"A crazy one, let's see." I thought about it for a couple of seconds. "Ok, here's one. True story, happened at LAX a couple of years ago. Ready?"

"Ready, ready." She said.

I told her the following. It is a true story, too.

About two years ago, I was sitting at the gate, waiting to board a flight from LA to Boston. A man sat down next to me. Early 50's, gray hair, thin. He was medium build, about 5' 10", white wearing a blue business suit. He had a suit coat and a briefcase.

He looked over at me and asked, "So, how's the conscience? Still having the murder dreams?"

"Excuse me?" I asked.

"The murder dreams. When I met you, you told me that you were having dreams about murdering a girl when you were a just a boy many years ago."

"I've never met you." I said.

"Yes sir, you have. We met about 14 months ago right here at this gate. I was sitting alone and you sat beside me and we got to talking. I told you that I never sleep when I come to LA because of the time change and you said the same thing happens to you when you go east. Then you told me about the dreams you had been having. You said you were having recurring dreams about killing a little girl with a rock. It was very detailed, your description of the whole thing."

"That couldn't have been me. That's totally insane." I told him.

"Insane, that's what I thought as I listened to you. I couldn't look at you because your eyes were swimming in your head. I didn't know what to do. I wanted to leave but you were intent on telling the story, so I just sat and listened."

"And I told you that I killed a little girl?"

"You said you had recurring dreams about killing a little girl with a rock in the park near an apartment building you used to live in when you were very young. You never said you killed the girl, no! You said you had the same dream over and over. You said you would dream of walking through the park down a hill to a small creek you used to go to all the time. You said in the dream, you knew why you were walking down there and the closer you got to the creek, the more frightened you became. You said the dream always ended the same way, you would get near the creek and see the little girl face down in the water, left arm at her side, right arm straight out like she was waving. You said you knew she was dead and you had killed her. You wanted to hide or run away but couldn't move from the spot even though your back was now to the girl's body, you knew she was still there. Then you said you heard voices. You said you knew it was your parents arguing and you thought they were arguing about their divorce but you somehow knew that they were really arguing about how to tell the mother of the little girl you had killed. Then you would wake up."

"I told you this, at this airport, several months ago?" I asked him.

"Yes. You said the girl lived down the street from you. Her name was Laura or Ann. I forget which. But you said you had been having this dream a lot and thought it was because one day she and her family moved away while you were at summer camp and you were mad about it and perhaps now you were processing the fact that you were mad about her leaving because you had a crush on her. Then I said you should maybe see a shrink and you said, 'Why do I need a shrink when I have you?' and then we both laughed. I said I hoped you stopped having the dreams and you didn't say anything. I got up to make some calls and didn't see you again until now. Oh, also, you said that in the dream, the sky was overcast."

"Well I don't remember this but thanks for the trip down memory lane, have a nice flight." I told him and then I got up and sat at another gate that was empty. I didn't see him on the flight and I've never seen him since.

"That happened?" she asked.

"Just like that." I told her.

"Talk about projecting. That's scary like that Truman Capote short story Miriam!" she said.

"Miriam destroyed me. You like Truman Capote?" I asked.

"Love. Truman. Capote." She answered.

"Can I hang out with you all the time?" I asked her, I felt like a little kid.

"I think you better." She said.

And that was that. We have been together ever since. You know how you hear men say when talking about their new wives or girlfriend, that they're the happiest man in the world? That's how I feel.

Quite simply, she is the miracle of my life.

She's also the only person I have ever confessed to.

I did in fact, kill a girl named Laura with a stone in 1968.

There was a park across the street from the apartment where my mother and I lived. I went there almost every day. Laura and I went to the same public school a few blocks away from where we lived. She used to follow me around and I pretended that I didn't like her but really, I did.

One day, after school, we were walking in the alley behind the apartment building and stopped at the backyard of a woman who had a lot of cats.

Most of them were feral and they fought. Their eyes were often closed from some infection. The woman had a deep accent, I don't know where she was from. Anyway, I used to go back there a lot and look at the cats. You couldn't get too close to them before they'd run away. They loved her though, she had the food. I would watch from my window, she would come out with pie tins of food and cats would materialize from everywhere.

Anyway, one day Laura and I were walking by the cat lady's yard and there was a kitten sleeping on the ground next to the fence. I picked up a rock, stood over the kitten and smashed in its head. I don't know why. I remember there was blood in the kitten's mouth and its teeth were very small and dirt was sticking to the kitten's tongue.

Laura didn't say anything. She just stood there. I told her we should bury the kitten in the park.

We walked to the park with the dead kitten and went down the hill to this creek I went to all the time. We got down to the edge of the creek and she knelt down to look at the water or something and I put down the kitten and picked up a stone I could barely hold and kind of leaned over her and dropped it. The stone hit her on the back of her head and right shoulder. She slumped forward and into the water. She was face first, left hand at her side and right arm out straight. She didn't move. I looked at her for a little while, threw the kitten into the water and went home.

The next day we got out of school early because her body was found and they wanted all the children in the neighborhood at their homes. I remember my mother coming to the school and taking me home by the arm, even though the school was a block away from our apartment.

Later on that evening, my father came over from his house across town to talk with my mother. I walked into the living room in my pajamas, surprised to see my dad because usually I only saw him on the weekends. I said, "Hi dad." He said, "Go to sleep. Your mother and I are talking." I went back to my room and that's when I heard them arguing. My mother wanted to pull me out of that school and move out of the neighborhood because she was afraid that I would get killed like Laura. My dad was trying to calm her down I guess but she was pretty hysterical.

So, about a week later, we moved. We moved about a mile across the city and I got sent to a private school out in the suburbs. No cops ever came to talk to me, no one ever asked me if I knew anything. Laura's parents moved away and my parents never spoke about it again.

It didn't occur to me that I had done anything all that bad but I did understand I shouldn't say anything about it because it would make my mother and father yell at each other. I always got upset when they did that. So, in order to keep them from yelling, I never said anything. After that, I just kind of buried it.

Years later, I realized the trouble I could get in if I ever told anyone and it was easy to never say a word about it. I don't know why I told that insane story to Tania. I guess I needed to at least say it to someone once.

Actually, there is no Tania. I don't have a girlfriend. I have never had an encounter like that on a plane but it's a dream of mine to some day meet a beautiful woman and talk about books and then live with her and be happy. Also, as an adult, I would never kill a person, or a kitten. That was a long time ago and I am truly sorry for what I did. And I do have those dreams. I always try and say I'm sorry or get her out of the water but in the dream, I can't speak or move. I'm not afraid of sleeping or having nightmares. I'm afraid of waking up. I'm afraid all the time. That's my problem.

You were the small brightly colored bird the boys incinerated their hearts upon. They loved you bitterly and called you a witch. You wanted to belong to someone. You found one but he tricked you and tore you like a sister's doll in a mean brother's hands and you became the hurricane child, spewing broken glass shards and cat blood. I tracked the blood drops through the snow and found you. You didn't fear me. We saw our-

selves in each other and holstered our weapons. Their conversations are dull and prey upon my intellect. They invade my senses and stupidly dominate my mind. It is a train platform and they have turned into a morgue for thought. If only I could lurk and limit my human contact to clandestine meetings in mystery filled nights of summer where insects gang the streetlights.

Their destination is not my destination. Will never be my destination. To them I will only give second hand information, facts they already know so they will absorb everything I say and quickly forget as they will think it all their creation. Thus, I will live invisibly amongst them. It is all the more pitiful that we are all going to the same place. My only separation from them will be the isolation I can maintain in my mind. And for this I must be strong and involve myself with nights of cold smoke, muted lights and strong commands barked from tired mouths.

Their conversations rain down like hammers from a high place. Their words jostle and crowd my brain. Perhaps it's their thoughts I am thinking now. Language is slavery. Understanding is self-imprisonment. I know what they are talking about. Their sentences straightjacket me. All their words in all their infinite combinations and permutations fill my pockets and shoes, they fill my lungs and throat to where I am breathing their words, their language, their lives and it's all so linear and headed to the well-traveled, overpopulated common ground of humanity I feel swept into the dustbin of existence, relegated to a life stuffed into a box and shelved anonymous and bricklike. I used to think my mind could save me. That my thoughts were the only things I needed to sustain me. My thoughts once staved off the excruciating banal existence of these people who stand hours in line for bread and meat. And now, they wait for this train.

Standing here on the platform, waiting to get on the train, the focus of my life becomes clear. Escape their prison of common thought. Escape the verbal procession that enslaves and smashes perception flat. I must see my life, what's left of it, in the gray light of duality, outward half truth and old dust long settled and unnoticed on window sills of backrooms. My new planet: The small mud and ice packed wood plank floor space I reserve for conducting ritualistic slow breath-by-breath suicide with them in the vast and strange land we are all heading towards when the soon arriving train takes us away.

This will be the only way for me to survive in the gulag. As the reality of living out my days in a concentration camp becomes more present, I will need to retreat and eventually disappear into this strange and secret solitary landscape.

They have tortured each other with systematic slaughter of thought to where none of them are aware their minds are nothing more than dumpsters of thrown away parts and worn out devices. Their conversations are heaving exchanges of worthless pieces of scrap metal. Their sound all around me, this generic drone of collapse, of evacuated ruins. Humanity's dead end.

There will be no revolution. There will be no cultural evolution. Just the constant exchange of scrap metal parts, memories of carcassed lives and elimination by starvation, execution, exhaustion and suicide in the gulag.

The self-proclaimed chosen have deemed us unworthy, so off we go into the cold and darkness, into small enclosures and animal panic. So here we wait. The train will come soon. I will surely throw myself onto the track to greet it and that will be the end of all thought.

In my mind I break away from the scrap heap and run into misted foreign nights, aromatic and endless. Never to be witnessed, never to be known. Free.

I'm ok with the fence around my house. I'm ok with my hand in the cookie jar. I'm ok with my white mind, my white lies and my doors locked. I'm ok knowing some go without. I'm ok that it's not me who gets his fingers smashed. I never pay in full. I'm getting away with it. I'm going to hold out

as long as I can. In my dreams, there's whispered threats, hands around my neck. At three in the morning my phone rings and a man tells me he's waiting for me outside the fence and wants kill me with his teeth, divide my body up amongst his friends and smoke my blood. Beautiful California, beautiful compound. Beautiful fence around me. The good life. We huddle together. Laid back and terrified. Hipsters with our hearts pounding in our throats. Gun in my mouth, emergency stash of Botox in the safe in case we can't get out of here for awhile. Three fathers in silence. Three fathers isolated in small quiet horror. Three fathers broken. #1. The father holds his daughter. Her fiancé is in an Army hospital. He has returned from war. He is legless. A portion of his face is gone. She is 22. It is her birthday today. As he holds his daughter, who weeps bitterly from her marrow, from her guts, from every moment of her young life, he becomes the eternal father. He becomes all fathers and now walks the ancient trail of the fathers before him who held their weeping daughters. #2. The father holds his screaming wife after they receive news their son has been killed. The father, alone in his horror where no family member or god can reach him now realizes after all the years of care and guidance, he was not there when his son needed him most. He knows he helped bring into this world, an innocent being who died in unimaginable pain. He knows he will bear the mark of all men who bury their sons. He knows the house will be dark and quiet now. He knows his son's pictures will be kept dustless by his wife. #3. The father walks the brown tiled hallway of the building that holds his son. He walks back and forth past the door to his son's room, waiting for him to awaken. His son cannot walk. His legs have been torn from his body and except for a foot still in a boot, turned into a fine red mist. His blood soaked the soil of a distant land. The father gave the world a beautiful boy who lies in a hospital bed with amputated stumps under white sheets and florescent lights, next to a small window that looks out at another building filled with amputated, charred and disfigured young men.

The small girl swings on a swing that hangs from a thick tree branch. There's nothing obstructing her view. It is very quiet. Everything around the tree has been destroyed. There are human bones with scraps of clothes at the foot of the tree. Her mother and father died in a Sarin gas attack. She lives with her blind grandmother. If you want a better world, blow this one up. Perhaps when the first blow to your head lands there will be a fraction of a second spent as your body adjusts. You have never been struck as an adult. No one, especially the common citizens, had previously dared to even look at you. Now they surround you, fascinated and enraged. That strange, heavy smell is your blood. A second blow lands on your left ear. The pain is amazing. Now you feel the hate. Someone hits you hard across the back of your head and you go down. The person who hit you likes people and animals and walks in the park. The person who hit you likes holidays and cake. There's nothing extraordinary about the person who hit you. There's nothing extraordinary about the people who encircle you. They're just people but they're inspired. They are inspired by you. Your actions have taken them across thresholds into territory they never knew existed. Before you lose consciousness, make sure to feel their hate. It's real and it's for you. It is their hate for you that has brought them together. It is your blood on the sidewalk that makes them see the world can be a better place and people can make a difference.

Big Boy: A Post-traumatic Hollywood legend. There's a billboard on Sunset Blvd. Billboard do have an enormous head complete with eyeballs. Billboard do say "Big Boy Mornings." Billboard also do say "Actual Size." Big Boy do say, "Girls are sweet—don't know nothing. Women are sour— nothing they don't know." Big Boy also do say, "Girls are sweet and women are sour. I'm burning mad hot watts and getting bigger by the hour." There's a bird on Big Boy's head. Big Boy's big black head is the orb-oracle for all the hardcore corner standing car hustling faggots on Santa

Monica Blvd. Smokin' pipe, smokin' crack, spittin' the product out the john's car window onto the floor of the alley behind Astro Burger. Straight up hustlers, hot pants stuffed with dick. Confrontation in full. Full-on street animals that make gangsters look like hollow-eyed doped bitches from the suburbs. Fuck 'em. Let's hit it. Let's rock. Let's die young on cheap lethal grinning skull street drugs. The death call. The true calling. Big Boy sees it all. Big Boy looks down onto the sun blasted concrete of the supermarket parking lot and watches the pock-marked stripper walking in slippers, sweat pants, rock and roll t-shirt, baseball cap and peroxide blond hair from the cheap piece-of-shithole litter box she shares with another stunt cunt moron hard case from the Mid-West who came out here fleeing daddy's hot mouth to do I don't know what the fuck but ended up working in a place where she gets her ass and knees filthy every night dancing in front of losers to Nine Inch Nails records. Big Boy looks down at this wolverine woman as she takes her tragic story ass to the market for a food, beer and cigarettes retox to energize for another smash-it-up on the bladed wheel. In the white sun haze, everyone looks like what they are—poisoned and full of death. LA—city of whores and fear and filth and death and ugliness and racist cops and cowards of all kinds. Big Boy Mornings purify on the mono AM. Big Boy billboards looking down at the stricken, at the fucked up, at the cursed, at the blood dripping from liquor store hold-ups, blood pouring from whatthefuckyoulookinatmuthafuckka gun up, gun out, gunned down dead for nothing, dead for seventy-five cent's worth of bullet in the head. Seventy-five second bleed out and no one saw a thing. Big Boy sees all. Big boy doesn't shed a tear. Big Boy knows it's all bullshit and these people are as expendable as anyone else and fear is the great equalizer of mankind. They're just like insects running around the hive and yeah, some are going to die so what. You can stop this madness any time you want but you like it. You get off on fear. It's the ill current that powers the city underneath Big Boy's ebony dome. The dome, the altar, where the birds come to shit like they do on Buddha. Big Boy looks down at the terrified scientologists as they scurry from the pod to the market to buy earthly supplies incognito before reality sinks its fangs in. Run space boy, the thetons are coming! Big Boy here today. Big Boy here tomorrow. You we're not too sure about. You don't have what it takes. You don't have a handle. You can't open the big doors. The people in those buildings who move all the pieces around, they speak a language you've never heard, that you'll never learn. They go where they want but at night they sleep in fear. They lie awake behind the wire, wondering how long until the people in the village come over the wall with knives and sticks and murder in their hearts. They know. Everyone knows. Everyone knows that it's only a matter of time before everything's on the street and there's no separation between the whores, the poets, the police and the elite. All the while Big Boy is big and flat, one hundred feet high overlooking the blvd. Big Boy do say, "Come to the city and try to be. Come to the city and bleed out for free."

It will never be love. It will always be something else mixed with setting suns, desperation and greed. I'm too broken for lust. I might as well tell you the truth. It sounds like my best lies anyway. It'll never be love. It's not like there's something better waiting for me somewhere else. And it's not like your eyes aren't open arms. I am a ghost town with a ribcage, every abandoned car. I heard every word you said. Tried to internalize your pleas as you cried. But it'll never be love. I'll reach for you when I need something that's pretty when it breaks. I knocked everything off the table to match the expression on your face when I told you I'm a stranger. Everything we touch belongs to someone else. I treat people like rentals. A man looking at the world through a punched out hole in a black wall.

After you were killed last June I quietly dismantled and disposed of my heart, parts of my nervous system and many of my thoughts. I did not yell or break anything. It was a subdued, slow and resolved process, as if I was

finally doing the one last thing that needed to be done. There was something familiar about it but I knew this was the last time. Had he not been so close to death he would have noticed how beautifully the sound of the oxen snorting nearby gently floated through the mist punctuated the dawn's stillness. So many early mornings he had sat and marveled at the utter perfection of it all. All had seemed good even though some of the locals wouldn't look him in the eye but cast their gaze downward and slightly to the side, he took no offense. He knew they were uneasy around foreigners. He had left America, the death machine, the homicidal maniac, the gasoline addicted, nation destroying culture killer. It had taken him years to come to the conclusion that he could no longer live there. One morning in the spring of his fortieth year, he sat in his living room, looked at his few possessions and decided it was time to leave America and never come back. It was not an anti-American sentiment that made him leave. It was exhaustion from a broken heart. America, love it or leave it. He loved America so he had to leave.

You get the last laugh. I tried and couldn't hack it. I didn't have what it takes to hang. It's obvious and the feeling of helplessness shames me to no end. People cause me pain. Trying to escape it, I have become addicted to suffocation. I have vacuum sealed myself into my thoughts. It's like living in a sunken ship. No air, yet I still breathe. In a room with one or one hundred I never get out of my skull. Years ago I would have been unable to imagine what the rest of my life was going to be like. Now I can. I am Josef Vissarionovich Dzhugashvili. My great great grandfather is the Great Stalin, the Man of Iron. I am tired of the bullshit. I am tired of my grandfather, Yevgeny Dzhugashvili, who holds me up like some kind of trophy. He never shuts up. I want to be left alone to smoke and torture animals but he's always here, taking me by the hand and showing me off as he struggles for street cred. He wants to restore the Soviet Union, run Vladimir Putin and all other "enemies of the people" as he calls them, out of the Kremlin. He's pathetic and I hate him.

I am only a child but smart enough to know my grandfather is a mere follower, someone who would have been sent to a gulag during Stalin's reign if only just to shut him up. Grandfather's father and Stalin's son, Yakov, was a prisoner in a German POW camp in WWII. Stalin was given the opportunity to trade him for a German officer and get Yakov home but he refused. Stalin didn't want to appear weak. Awesome! The fact that Stalin let my great grandfather die must get to Grandfather. It has to. Stalin let his own son die in a German camp and Grandfather still worships Stalin! I think it's brilliant. It is also a testament to what a great and powerful leader Stalin was. Grandfather is a suck up coward. I spit in his tea before I bring it to him. A dose of strychnine is what he deserves.

Stalin killed a lot of people. Grandfather tells anyone who will listen that the reports of mass killings of Soviet citizens is a pack of lies concocted by Khrushchev to demonize and belittle Stalin. Grandfather's whole life has been lived in the shadow of the Great Stalin. Grandfather spent his life working at a defense manufacturing plant always waiting to get fired, never wondering why he wasn't promoted. He spent his whole life trying to clean up Stalin's image. Lies and apologies are his stock and trade and he tells me to listen to him when he speaks. It's all I can do not to stab him in the eye.

It's obvious Grandfather doesn't see the good in being acknowledged as a descendent of the most brutal dictator in history. I think it's cool. Believe me, it gets me a lot of free lunches at school. No homework? No problem! I already have bitches lined up for when puberty hits.

Stalin was Time Magazine's Person of the Year in 1940. Bush was Time Magazine's Person of the Year in 2004. Americans are like Grandfather. Weak. My great great grandfather was a master's master. He starved his people to death, froze them, shot them, buried them alive and the survivors cried at his funeral. If President Bush had the balls to do this to his own people, the World Trade Center towers would still be standing. You understand if Stalin was in power right now, Osama bin Laden's skin would be carpet on the Kremlin floor and there wouldn't be a Koran in existence. There would be no Chechens and all those Saudi princes would be getting raped and tortured in Siberia.

Grandfather says a man like Stalin is born once in a thousand years. I will prove him wrong. I will come to power.

For a better life, Russians will let others freeze to death on the streets during our endless winters. They will fabricate, with great texture, depth and intricacy, long tales that expose the pettiness and shallowness of their neighbor, if only for some more heat and extra food rations. With the promise of the dream yet to be fulfilled, with their eyes set on what is to be theirs, so rightfully theirs, they will follow me. With souls captured by pure, all consuming avarice—they will follow me.

And even when their fathers and husbands never return from work and their apartments go cold and dark and families are turned out into the frozen streets, even when gulags and holding cells are filled well past capacity and men who have committed no crime are thrown in with the others and ultimately starved, worked or beaten to death and never heard from again—they will worship. They will believe in the dream with even greater fervor.

They will recognize all those who were executed, imprisoned or otherwise made to vanish as dangerous enemies of the people. Loss of a family member will bring them closer together, increase their level of fear and devotion. The will see me as an all-knowing, all-seeing god.

Every day when they rise, starving or fed, they will see that by the mere fact they are breathing, they are the chosen ones. They will know the ones who are no longer in evidence were the problem, the stones in the pathway that leads to the great, golden all radiant triumph that awaits all those who believe. That these enemies are now gone, will be to their great relief. They will obey. They will not question.

Oppression. The world cries out against those who oppress. Oppression is good. Oppression makes people feel part of something greater than themselves. Even in the midst of starvation and grey seasons of flattening misery they will look to the future and feel secure.

Look at Russia, a nation of brutes, thugs and peasants. Did you see the mess that was made when my people got a taste of freedom? Bedlam. Corruption from the streets to the Government level. Mafia running unchecked. Drug dealing in Red Square, like some vile American street corner. A cesspool of divergent thought and giddy, weakened peasants running around stupidly. Freedom makes order impossible. People cannot be trusted to take responsibility for their actions. Look at America.

Putin, an ant of a man, shut down news media outlets critical of his administration. How can anyone respect a man whose course of action is meted out in half-measures? That these media outlets were independently owned in the first place shows the world the weakness of Putin's grip. The fact that these disseminators of chaotic information are allowed to live at all tells me all I need to know about the great Putin. An ex-KGB man! When I come to power, he and his entire family will disappear. He will be purged from our history books and will never be spoken of again.

Many years of the decadent West have weakened my great country. Too many meals, not enough labor, not enough fear.

Gorbachev should have been executed long before the Berlin Wall came down. The Wall will come back. East Germany will be mine once again.

Only by absolute measures and fear can a leader truly lead. Fear works at all hours. Fear is the ultimate task master. Fear installs the police inside the mind of a man. He will be as close to self-governed as leadership needs him to be. Some say fear debilitates, breaks the spirit. Nothing could be further from the truth. The last thing a man needs is choice. Choice dizzies and stupefies a man. A man needs simple orders and the promise of ultimate consequences if all rules are not obeyed.

The strength of a nation can be evaluated by how much a man dares to think. The more he dares, the weaker the nation.

A year ago when I was three, I cut the throat of the family dog with a carving knife. The dog licked my hand as its blood soaked the backyard.

That was a great lesson to me. Those you oppress will worship your unchecked power. Those who fear you will never betray you. Their fear is their loyalty to you. Fear is better than love.

To still the talk of the intellectuals and agitators, whose annoying clamor is like a group of school girls in spring, answer these questions: Why is the great America still afraid of Russia? Why does Russia have no fear whatsoever of America? Because even after fifty years of bad leadership, deep inside the Russian heart is the desire to follow. The desire to freeze and starve, to go without and stand in long lines. They know that only suffering will bring them to greatness. Only great suffering and loss allows them a slight reprieve from their inherent guilt. They know what they are.

Too many choices and too much perceived freedom makes people arrogant, neurotic and foolish. It makes them dull and lazy. Freedom, even the idea of it, corrupts and weakens a nation. Look at what it did to the turgid and lumbering America! Listen to the Americans all talking at once! Every one of them a leader, every one of them so informed. Like yapping dogs they never cease. Their overabundance of imagined courage is nothing but stupidity running amok. Their lack of respect for authority, this laughable contempt they take with them everywhere like it's their birthright is the mark of a nation that doesn't understand the true and basic meaning of authority. They fear each other but they don't fear authority. Without this clear understanding derived from and maintained by constant displays of absolute and brutal force, no population will ever truly regard authority and authority figures in the correct manner. Only when authority is autonomous and omnipotent does it serve its purpose.

The Americans have contempt for authority and the state. They run wild in the streets like animals. They call this decadent farce freedom when it is in fact a wretched state of chaos. Their strutting pomposity is pathetic as it is transparent.

Only when a nation fears its officials and authority figures, only when citizens have absolute proof of drastic and immediate punishment that results from any infraction or transgression of the penal code, real or perceived, will their nation be truly strong. That the Death Penalty is not mandatory in all parts of America, that there's even a waiting period, Death Row as they call it, shows the rest of the world that America is weak. Protesters say sometimes someone who isn't guilty is executed. Yes. The occasional killing of an innocent is a strong deterrent. If all Death Row inmates were executed in a single day, the crime rate in America would drop noticeably. If a few people were taken from street corners and publicly executed for no given reason, the crime rate would drop even more. But America never does what it needs to be strong. I will show them.

It is this unwavering and all crushing authority and power that has elevated my great great grandfather, Josef Vissarionovich Dzhugashvili, otherwise known all over the world as Stalin, to such a great height that for all generations to come, he will be seen as the greatest leader mankind has ever known.

Stalin, the Father of our great nation is the only man in the world's history to ever lead a nation correctly. He was a great knower of the human heart. He held an entire nation and a good part of the world in his grip. As country after country fell to our mighty army, its people were ecstatic and relieved to be stabilized and given purpose to their lives. The Hungarians must have been thrilled to see Soviet tanks thunder into Budapest. The Hungarians were no doubt overjoyed to know that finally in their life time they would know the meaning of true leadership and live under its uncompromising perfection in one yielding, exhausted surrender and turnover of hundreds of millions of dollars to Stalin. What were those filthy fascists thinking they were going to do with the money?! Freedom was obviously too heavy a weight for the disgusting Hungarians to bear.

In any society where there is the slightest trace of freedom, you will find unhappiness and uncertainty. The crushing disappointment when their eggshell thin illusion is shattered by a knock on their door at four hours past midnight and a family dutifully lines up to kiss poppa goodbye one last time as he is lead away into the cold and dark mystery of disappearance, never to be seen again. And that's the lesson, the result of this intoxicating inhalation of hope and hapless dash towards the siren-song of freedom—someone always knows better, knows more. So, just stop hoping and let the state take care of things. Realize your place in the greatness of the silent and immovable power. Rejoice that you are a small and unimportant part of something huge and important that has been assembled by those who know better, who know more.

For a nation to be strong, the entire population must be broken. It must be broken spiritually, it must be rendered godless and powerless so there is no distraction.

In this environment there are no coups or uprisings. There is no disgruntled muttering at the dinner table or whispered conversations in beds at night about what is "wrong." In this environment, there are no wrong thoughts because no one knows to think them and those few who do, don't dare.

The perfect state of order and outer calm can only be achieved by the systematic crippling and destruction of the individual.

Perhaps the most effective method of neutralizing the threat of freethinkers and agitators is by random punishment of innocent people. When father doesn't return home from work, it is obvious to all that he has done something wrong and is paying the price for this. What did he do?! The man's family ransack their beleaguered and muddled brains trying to figure it out. "He seemed like such a good man! Not all that smart, no! But he worked hard. Even when he was hardly able to get out of bed, he went in to work his sixteen hour shift. What was it he did? Am I unknowingly doing it too? Am I to be next? What are the neighbors thinking? Are they the ones who turned in Poppa?"

They stay in their apartments. They avoid eye contact. They never speak to strangers. They only speak of the greatness of their leader and the strength of the state and their willingness to give all. They speak loudly at the market about the virtues of the state hoping all hear what a good and obedient one the owner of the voice is. Someone's always listening. Someone's always watching. Someone always knows better, knows more.

Now people suspect and distrust each other and this is good. Everyone gets their work done and no one looks around much further than the ground directly in front of them. They trust no one. They fear and distrust each other. They go to work. And thus, a nation grows strong. Only in their deepest thoughts do they wonder and soon they will not even wonder there. There's only work and more work to celebrate this life in the paradise that the Great One has so lovingly provided for them all.

A few years in, their own thoughts are so long gone they don't remember what it was like to have such thoughts or if they ever had them at all. Now all efforts are put to the long term good of the great nation. A generation will toil ceaselessly so another generation can have the privilege to do the same. The individual is destroyed and people become "The People."

If America could grasp these concepts and act on them, they would be the strongest nation the world. Think about it. There would be no racism, no class struggle, no elitism and no intellectuals running around, screwing things up with their shrill voices and effeminate posturing. But thankfully, they are hopelessly lost in their world of ambition and half-truths and the world hates them for it.

The West has always feared Russia. Even at its most impoverished, even when it was run by the idiot pig Khrushchev or the liberal faggot Gorbechov, the West has always feared us. But most importantly, America, the great paper tiger of the modern world, the spoiled child—has always feared Russia.

America has always resented our placement of the first man in space, Yuri Gagarin and the first woman in space, Valentina Tereshkova. They tried vainly to show the world they landed on the moon but we have the surveillance tapes of NASA shooting the landing footage in the American desert. We killed the Kennedy's. When I come to power, the world will see this footage. There's over one hundred hours of it. But this is nothing.

America has lied through its teeth to its people and to the world for decades. It's time for America to pay. It's time for America to pay more. It's time for America to learn the strength found in suffering. It's time for Americans to learn how cold the winter can be. I will unmask America to the world. I will show them. I will show them all.

The American president wavers back and forth on what measures to employ to fight the forces that walked right into his country and used American planes to destroy major landmarks and take thousands of lives. The fact that the Middle East exists at all now is nothing more than a testament to this man's inability to lead men to battle and a nation to its ultimate greatness. A war is not won by standing around and getting killed. A war is won by killing everyone who is not on your side and taking what was once theirs. It's when you call it something else and operate on a lie that you needlessly sacrifice your soldiers in the way President Bush has.

Arrogance, fear of confrontation and the inability to do what needs to be done has always made America despicable to me. Over and over again, America shows itself to be cowards. From Vietnam to Desert Storm they resisted every opportunity to win decisively and by doing that, lost every conflict they've ever engaged in. While their countrymen were in Vietnam, what did millions of Americans do? They dodged the draft! They held protest marches! They held hands and sang songs. That these people were not arrested and executed immediately tells me all I need to know about America. It will be mine.

Now the world knows that America is unable to defend itself. Now the world knows that America is not to be feared. The sheet has fallen off the Great America, the jewel in the crown of the Western World only to reveal a nation of soft bellied, terrified people living on borrowed time. A nation afraid to fight. A nation unable to do what it must to defend its borders and protect its interests. This will not be the fate that befalls my country when I come to power.

I will destroy Islam. Their mosques, their books, their entire history will be erased. In three generations the world's largest religion will no longer exist in practice, thought, printed page, cloistered darkness, on any wall or in any heart. Words of the Koran will not hang on the lips of trembling Mullahs and fervent devotees because they will all be destroyed. Their countries will be flattened. Their people will be exterminated. Their mighty Allah will not lead them to fortune. Their mighty Allah is nothing. Their arrogance and idiotic devotion will matter not a bit. They will be crushed like ants whilst kneeling on their prayer mats. Osama bin Laden and his hopeless army of faggots marching around the mountains of Afghanistan, so proud that the mighty Allah gave them the strength to strike America, will all die.

I will vaporize Afghanistan, Pakistan, Saudi Arabia and India in a week. North Korean flesh will melt off bone. China will do nothing to help their friends across the Yalu river. They know better. At the end of the day, the Chinese and the North Koreans and especially the Americans, are cowards. It is only a matter of time until the world is mine.

Interviews in the Fleshy World or Microdramas of the Wounded Play Out.

"If I told you I loved you, walked 100 miles to hear you say my name, ate ten pounds of sand, bled from my eyes, would you take the wound away?"

"When I envision the bullet crashing through my skull, I wonder if there would be a second between its exit and mine where I would feel unwounded. I wonder what that impossible to reach world would be like to live in and if I could somehow squeeze a compressed and ecstatic life time into that fraction of a second."

"Without the wound I would be no one, nowhere, without sorrow, without a song. My paint would run dry, my blood would thicken and my words would be ash falling back into the mouth of a dead volcano."

"She was running from something. I was running from something. We ran into each other, looked at each other's wounds and felt safe together. We protected ourselves with dope. We cleaned up together and never saw each other again. I am running from something. I..." (tape runs out).

"Years ago I went out with a woman who only enjoyed sex in a few positions. Memories of her Uncle ruined her for anything else. Every once in awhile she would stop me and say, 'No, that's too much like my uncle,' and we would stop. It was very sad. We would lie still for awhile and then go to sleep."

"I just wish there was a way around it all as years pass and perception grows more exacting and truths more inescapable. I pull myself though time season by season. In Autumn, I tell myself to keep on until Spring. In Spring, I tell myself that Autumn will be beautiful. I graffiti the wound with a smile and now and then it sticks for awhile, but only because I see yours."

I knew that only by leaving everything familiar would real life truly start for me. I had to break all ties and move far away. Brutality and sadness were all I was leaving behind so the choice was clear. So much sadness and pain in the rearview. It hurt so much to leave them. Some of the people I knew were truly wonderful. I know I will think of them for the rest of my life. The streets of my hometown I will never walk on again, just thinking of them now brings tears to my eyes but I had to go. K, my good friend. I am leaving this letter at the American Embassy, hoping you will check in before you leave the country. I don't know when you will get this and only hope that no great harm has befallen you. It's been months since I've heard from you and was only able to get bits of information as to your state and whereabouts. I was told you are somewhere in the mountains waiting for rainy season to start so you can make a discreet exit. No one in any of the bars will tell me exactly why you left so quickly. I got the distinct feeling that being persistent with my questions was endangering my own situation, which as you know, is always dodgy around here so I stopped.

I imagine by the time you get this letter (and I am going to remain optimistic and say that you will), you will want to know what happened to all your possessions. Here's what I was able to find out: The river dried up and your boat sat in the mud for about five days. The boat was looted and set on fire by some of the locals who said it was cursed because you brought evil to it (!) As you probably surmised, they never liked you and even though you lived amongst them for years and learned their language, they never trusted you. I can't think any of this surprises you my friend.

The American, where can he go where he's not hated? He's safe nowhere. Not in America, not in the world. You know what they say, once a foreigner, always a foreigner. They ransacked your room and were angry that they found nothing of value. You could have at least left them some candles, some soap! I know why you had to leave, I understand. I am not long for this place myself. I refuse to believe that we bring this curse upon ourselves. I will not believe that all Americans are lost in the world. I will hold out hope there are those still living in America who are brave enough to face the oppressors and some day overthrow the regime. I know I no longer have the strength of will. It hurts to think that from this great distance, America still breaks my heart. What it could have been and will never be is what hurts the most.

When I think of all the times and places we have crossed paths, all the years we have spent away from America, I wonder if we'll ever get back there. It's not even time spent away from America at this point, it's just our lives now. Time spent back there would only be time spent away from the world. There's nothing for me there. It's such a sad and polluted land. I will take my chances out here for as long as I can hold out. America broke my heart all those years ago when I knew I had to leave. I am better now and live for good nights of sleep in dry seasons and water that doesn't make me sick.

Also, all your papers, manuscripts and notes were thrown out. If I had arrived here a day earlier I could have perhaps recovered some of the work but alas, it's all gone now. I suspect you anticipated all this and it makes me respect you all the more.

Alright my friend, I am off. If you get this, please ask for me at the Triumph Hotel as I will be there for some days trying to get my papers straightened out so I can get out of here.

Take care old friend. —AR

The Unhappy Family. When I look back, it's not with anger but with sadness at the shambles of us. That we can't go back and fix the past so we wouldn't have to dwell in the ruins of it now. In my mind I have invented a past for us that is free of the fear and uncertainty that held us to tightly in its grip. This invented past is a brief, blank space, a momentary fragment of non-existence. For a black vacuumed moment, we never were and in that moment we are not isolated and confused and alienated from ourselves or each other. But of course it does not work. The idea that I must wait for you to die so I can live is not useful to me. The black space of non existence provides no relief. So I remember the only facts I need. I remember I am a soldier and the past is a village I incinerated and I am miles up river and behind the tree line.

And soon all but little few will be scraped away. What shall remain? Ruin, rats and rusty nails. Who shall love us? None but the coughing wind and the sickened, receding tide. This is what happens to the cold handed who sit alone in small rooms. Poor, poor sun. It too has left us. What, no songs to sing? No. The radio chewed its cord off to be free. Alas. I am mainlining

amniotic fluid in the hope that something lives inside me. I don't want anything, not even a parasite to die now. My only child, long gone, suffered oligohydramnios during my pregnancy. All of our men have gone to war. If they ever do come home, I want there to be something for them to come back to. It's so hard to be here and know. One day it started. It seems like a life ago. I will refer to this day as Day One. On Day One, I was cleaning the floor of a closet space my wife and I rarely use. On this day while cleaning, I discovered the first sign of its arrival. It was a drop of thick black liquid, not unlike paint. This was the first proof that it was here.

Before Day One, there were moments when my wife and I would sit in the living room in the early evening and everything I saw and said was imbued with a drained, dissipated sense of final destination and vague desolation. It was barely noticeable but inescapable. The light coming in through the windows had a wan, lifeless, gently oppressive cast. Our conversations were sporadic and disembodied, like they had been spooned from cans. They hung like old smoke. Our words were nothing more than combinations, comments on what the other had just said. I knew it was more than years of marriage dulling the senses. It was a feeling but it registered like fact. Something was coming.

I wondered if anyone else had noticed. At my job everyone seemed normal. They were friendly and regarded me in the usual fashion. I did notice the overhead lights in the coffee lounge had a greyness about them I had not noticed before. I turned them off and on a few times and they fired up fine but they still looked greyer than any florescent lights I had ever seen. In the days preceding Day One, I noticed by early afternoon, the sunlight coming in through the windows at the office made me think they were slightly tinted but they weren't. The light coming in was actually gray. There was a feeling of apprehension in my stomach at all times. I would forget to breathe. I sat in my office thinking of nothing for lack of ability to concentrate on anything and heard someone nervously clear their throat. Someone had been standing in front of me. I would apologize and jokingly say I was lost in thought and the person would tell me I had been looking them right in the eye for at least half a minute.

During the nights leading up to Day One I started having two recurring dreams.

In the first dream I am standing on the bank of a large cement aqueduct. It looks like a section of the LA riverbed. The sky is grey but cloudless. My breathing is slightly labored. My mouth and throat feel coated with a thin layer of a metallic tasting substance. From my left, the sound of static or white noise steadily grows louder until it reaches a medium level, stops increasing and remains constant. I do not move my head. And then it comes. A boiling wall of black liquid crashes down the aqueduct. The liquid wall is soundless as it comes closer. The static I am hearing remains constant and seems to have no relation to the liquid. The wall has passed me now and I look to my right. The black line of liquid is filling the aqueduct as far as I can see. I look down and the level of the liquid has come to the top of the cement and is now spilling over onto the dirt I am standing on. The liquid touches my shoes. I wake up.

In the second dream I walk out the back door of the house and into the backyard which is long and narrow, about four car lanes wide. A man in a black suit and tie with a white shirt is standing at the bottom of the aqueduct several yards away from me. I do not fear him. I walk down a flight of stairs cut into the wall of the aqueduct and walk towards him. I notice the sky is grey and cloudless. There's no sign of the sun besides the fact that it's light enough to see but it seems like the light is from another source. I also notice that there are no houses in sight. There is no sound. I can't hear the sound of my breathing. I walk up to the man and stop in front of him. He is of normal height and build. He is not threatening to me. I stand in front him and he looks at me and then looks down at the cement. He drops to one knee and points his right index finger at the ground. I see a drop of black liquid. The man looks up at me to see if I have noticed. I look at him and nod. He stands up and I turn and walk back towards the house. At some point before I get to there I wake up.

I have never told my wife about the dreams. In the days leading up to Day One, we had been growing quieter around each other. Neither of us have many friends so the hours spent at the house were not interrupted by phone calls or visitors. We just sat and blankly passed time. Entire weekends would go by, groceries unbought, errands unattended to. When we did speak, it was calm and rational but impersonal and professional. Sitting in the living room with her reminded me of sitting near a stranger in the lobby of a hotel early in the morning while waiting for the airport shuttle.

The dreams would wake me up but not in a state of panic or unrest. I would just open my eyes. I do remember it would be completely dark when I woke up which made me wonder whether I was really awake or still dreaming. One time I thought perhaps my eyeballs were solid black marbles and it was light out but I could no longer see. I remember thinking to myself you could say you can't see because it's too dark or you could say you're seeing the darkness very well.

And then Day One came. The black liquid had reached the reality of my waking state when I cleaned it off the floor. I smelled it to see if it might be paint or tar or something I could recognize but it was completely odorless.

On Day Two I went back to the spot where I found the drop of black liquid on Day One. There was another drop in the exact same place. I got a foot ladder and looked at the ceiling over the area of the drop. I saw no holes, cracks or sign of anything unusual. I cleared the drop with my index finger and smelled the liquid and again, it was odorless. The area beneath the drop had no crack or hole. It was as if it had been placed there with an eye dropper.

On the morning of Day Three, it occurred to me the dreams had stopped on the night of Day One. It was as if the dream had been transported to reality.

Day Three was a Monday. I went to work. Everything was normal except for the light, which still had a grey tint.

Upon arriving home I went directly to the closet to see if the drop was in its usual spot. My wife was in the closet, looking for a jigsaw puzzle. She said hello to me as if we were two shoppers in a narrow aisle. After she had gone, I looked at the spot. The black liquid was there but it looked like at least a teaspoon's worth. I cleaned it off the floor with a piece of tissue paper. I wondered why she had not seen the spot or at least stepped in it. I wondered if she had put the liquid there but I can't think why she would do such a thing.

In the living room that night, all the ceiling track lights were on as well as the lamps but it was still hard to read a magazine. The pages seemed to be an off-white color and the type seemed to be out of focus. My wife's voice sounded muffled and there was a slight hissing sound in my ears like steam escaping from a cracked pipe.

By my calculation, it is now Day One Hundred and Eighteen. I clean the ever widening spot of black liquid. I showed the spot to my wife several weeks ago and all she said was, "Maybe it's birds. Maybe it's dead birds." Since then we don't talk about the spot of black liquid.

I have noticed a lot of dead birds on the way to work. In the dark and long nights I have noticed my wife sleeps soundly but it's hard to tell she's breathing. If I happen to brush against her, she will jerk her upper back and take a sharp, convulsive breath, like someone being revived.

Two nights ago my wife walked by me and said, "I'm going to hang myself, care to join me?" Her father was the super in the apartment building she and her family lived in. He hanged himself in the laundry room when she was fourteen.

It's here now. Whatever it is. It's here and has taken silent residence in my life. I used to wonder what the future held for me, now it's just about what's in front of me. I can't tell you what I did at work today or what I had for dinner last night or the difference in taste between salt and sugar. I don't know if I went to work last week. I do remember yesterday. I saw people in the neighborhood putting up flyers for their lost pets. Whatever was coming is now here.

Why does it always include either suicide or some other negation of self or world? They hurt to know, people. It hurts to know them. I'd rather not. I like them but they hurt. "A few more years and I'm out." Is the jab of morphine in my mind's blood. Just a few more years of pain and then something else. There's a desert in my room. There's a pit in the middle. My bed's at the bottom. I sleep with trash and the animals who have fallen in and were unable to escape. So far, it's a dog, a deer and a bird that drags its left wing. I dream I'm asleep dreaming. I put the left side of my face on the pillow, curl into the fetal position and shoot a bullet into my mouth. In the dream I wake up from the dream and see that I've just shot the trapped deer in its mouth instead of myself. I wake up from the dream and remember where I am. I am in the Amerikan vacuum. Cut off and isolated from other Amerikaners and the rest of the world. I am choked off by pavement and stores. The Amerikaners don't know where their food comes from but it keeps coming and they can't eat it fast enough to stem the flow. Every sign for every fast food agency advertises bigger and cheaper. Almost daring the Amerikaner to step up and try and eat it all. Freedom holds them hostage. A sense of entitlement they're unaware of or don't care to acknowledge makes them headstrong and catastrophically brave. The Amerikaner is easy to kill. Colorful, loud and slow moving, telegraphs every intention with a sense of duty to let everyone know. The bottom line is unheeded. Warnings from scientists, environmentalists and financial advisors are waved aside with ignorant contempt. The food is bad. The water is dirty. The Amerikaner can't see the real enemy. They look everywhere but where they should. They make it up to suit their ever-changing moods. All nonwhites are token nonwhites. All women are token nonwhites. Amerikaners are the self-fatted calves shunted off from the world, walking unescorted onto the belt enticed by bad music, fatted food and drugs. You need a lot of chemicals to wake them up and snap them out of their komalaktik state of the union. But it's not a union they have. It's an entanglement. It's broken treaties and infected blankets. It's men sleeping under highway overpasses. It's a bone lodged in the throat. It's nymphomaniacs holding each other at gunpoint and calling it art or just another day of annihilation. Amerikaners cut off like a belted arm full of narcotic saturated blood. They host many parasites so they're always hungry and thirsty, always eating and drinking but never full or quenched. Always acquiring but never satisfied. Happiness is rarely found but items are bought and sold nonstop. Amerika is turgid with resources but many feel empty. The privileged are terrified. The ingratiated feel alienated. The alienated feel ingratiated by alienation, bus stops, handouts and the crawlspaces in which they live out their character arcs on the outer rings of psychosis that radiates from the city centers like vomit from a tilt-a-whirl. Work hard and get stuff so you can worry about the stuff and work harder to protect what you've worked so hard for. The Amerikaner buys items to indicate to others that he's a more prominent and dominant slave to the grind. In no other culture in the world is this arduous task tackled with more single-minded intensity. Amerikaners are inspired to build mountains so big they cannot be climbed and achieve the unachievable so the rest of the world knows its place. Whatever achievements they might accomplish are small in comparison and will engender patronizing, over enthusiastic accolades from the superior ones like a grandson who won the science prize or that dog who can catch the frisbee every time.

Birth of Dog Eater. Born into mother father cross town loathing. Learned lessons early. Life will be all you can stand. Life will be solitude and pain. Life will be bright with moments of violence and inequality. Dog Eater acclimated to the world of confrontation and pain until there was nothing but the way things are. Dog Eater sought to acquire self knowledge and self control. Dog Eater walked into the maelstrom and quickly learned the trade routes.

Dog Eater saw Dog Eater blood. Tasted it. Overcame the barriers that separates one from self possession: revulsion, innocence, denial and moral restraint. The ability to withstand pain and commit acts of explosive and overwhelming violence with efficiency and zero hesitation were hard won strengths. Almost immediately Dog Eater realized most live under some kind of oppression. They need and trust it. They need boundaries set by others because for many, there's a cutoff point where they need to relinquish control. Dog Eater knew early on there were those who wait for someone to hit that eventual threshold dictated by a god, lack of resolve or well placed propaganda. They wait and when the victim of oppression hits the wall, the oppressor is there with tepid culture, alcohol, slippery employment opportunities and credit to sooth, addict and entrap. They call it real life and they approach it with grim and resigned determination. A life for many. Not for Dog Eater. Into the river of consequence went Dog Eater. Breaking the spines of one lie after another, Dog Eater saw there was only truth and that which stands in the way of truth. Truth is not painful. Flinching from it is. Where you're at is where you are and all is good. **Dog Eater and the Scarred Woman**. A man she worked with slashed her face with a box cutter when she was coming out of her apartment three years ago. She had turned him down twice when he asked her out. He stalked her for a month and when she was on her way to the gym one evening he walked up to her, brought the blade down her left cheek hard and ran. He was never caught. From under the hard packed filth of the city streets, through tired nights of dead rooms and suicide's blackened entrance wounds came Dog Eater. With a blade more wicked than the first day of spring, Dog Eater took an ear and both thumbs from the good woman's attacker and ate them in front of the man as he screamed, vomited and went into shock. Not for revenge you fucking hippy piece of shit! Fuck revenge! Just kill! Just maim like President Coward orders young men to do in distant deserts. Not for love! Fuck love! Love is for weeping mothers rubbing the stumps of their son's legs! Dog Eater will gut and clean you like a ten point buck after hacking your family to pieces. Dog Eater will wash in your blood as your armies kill in foreign lands. Dog Eater will burn your house to the ground and send your hands in a box to your mother-in-law as Muslim women scream in agony as their husbands are torn apart by bullets. The Scarred Woman wears a scarf to cover her face. She is sickened when she looks in the mirror. She has told the police three times now she honestly doesn't know who could have done this to her. She is relieved the man who made her nervous at her place of work suddenly quit. No one takes the scarf from her face and brushes the scar with their lips and tells her she's so beautiful. No one shoots the moon in the face. No one locks crime in a cage and tells it to push the pedal for the biscuit. Dog Eater will tell her she's beautiful. Dog Eater will kiss her. Dog Eater will not tell the Scarred Woman why his tongue tastes like blood. Dog Eater will re-create Michelangelo's painting on the ceiling of the Sistine Chapel with your entrails. **Dog Eater Theme.** From underneath I come. Subhuman, subcanine, subcontempt. My bones are crooked from being broken so many times. Violence has made them strong. My flesh is scarred and burned and stronger for it. It is superior to flesh that has never been split nor seared. Your brutality has taught me well, made me strong and separated me from fear of pain. I want death more than you want life. You have taught me well. You taught me to sleep in the cold, eat dirt covered scraps and drink filthy water. You taught me my life is worth nothing and in that, I have learned that yours isn't either and so I push my ribcage against the toe of your boot when you come to visit. You can't kill alone. I can. I eat what I kill. I am always hungry. I can kill you. I can eat your brains. **Dog Eater and the Inquisition.** *What say you, Dog Eater? Time to arise, time to respond to provocation, time to recoil but eventually submit to authority. Up, up Dog Eater!* What say me Inquisitor? My eyes see! They search around! For what, you ask? So many questions, so many demands! Why, I'm looking for something to beat your brains out with. I'm looking for a sharp instrument to cut your ears off with so that I may wear them around my neck. Never stare into the eyes of the assassin, Inquisitor. Never underestimate the strength of the scarred survivors of your torture houses. We are alive and will watch the blood come from your mouth. Every bit of torture we endured was a lesson learned, a weapon loaded and holstered. What was done to us will be done to you. **Dog Eater and Cracker**. Emmet Till's body is out of the ground and being examined. Emmet Till's assassins are now dead. Dog Eater will find the children of the assassins and eat their eyes one at a time so they can see. So they can see! Dog Eater can smell Cracker. Dog Eater can sniff out America's cowardice and denial. Cracker can't seem to evolve. Dog Eater will evolve Cracker. Cracker's eyes will come out one by one. Cracker will scream. Cracker will get a history lesson. Cracker will be able to figure out the following equation: Cracker kill + body get dug up = Cracker lose eyes. The lesson? Cracker is born to walk this earth blind. Cracker is born to start car in garage, sit in the front seat and die. Cracker is born to kill his kids and then blow his brains out. Cracker is born to cut his cracker bitch wife's body down from the rafter she hung herself from. Emmet Till died for nothing and so will Cracker. Emmet Till died once. Cracker will die over and over. Fertilize southern fields of cotton with ground Cracker bones. Feed Cracker guts to the crows and turkey vultures. It's a new day so let Dog Eater come in and lynch a Cracker! Dog Eater will whisper in your ear while you're asleep. When you wake up, you will light incense and rub Buddha's belly. You will go to Salt Lake City, drop LSD and then drop LDS as they spill from their churches, burning and screaming. **Dog Eater and Love**. If Dog Eater chopped off a finger for every woman Dog Eater ever loved, Dog Eater would have the same amount Dog Eater has now. Ten scarred and smashed fingers. From under the weight of heaving and heartbroken humans, mothers torn from their sons by the President Coward, miles distant from the lonely and crushed by love, Dog Eater walks alone untouched by the misery of millions. Ten fingers. Dog Eater rises early and stays up late. Dog Eater sees children with their parents and only sees future soldiers and those who will mourn their mutilation and death. Love is for those ready to lose. Love is for those who fear the darkness outside the fire's light. Dog Eater sees this and knows only discipline, repetition and application to the task will separate one from those who love, those who suffer at the hands of cowards and liars. Dog Eater is sick of lies and cowardice. Dog Eater knows that pain and confrontation are Dog Eater's friends. Cold, isolation, existence in deserted and ruined spaces strengthen Dog Eater. Missing no one, mourning no one only add to Dog Eater's ability to see and think clearly. Dog Eater knows those who sacrifice time and energy spent on love and the misery that comes with it are happy to lose because they fear triumph and don't know what to do with time spent undeterred by the day-to-day denial they wallow in as they cling to relationships that only want to pull apart. Fear brings them together and contempt separates them. How long will they hold out? This is no concern of Dog Eater's. **Dog Eater and the Inquisition.** *What say you, Dog Eater?* With joy and burning hatred I spit a mouthful of blood, hair and part of your ear on the floor to show you I am alive and free and fearless and expect to be executed by one of the cowards whose mind and spirit you've conquered and broken. With clear eye and unceasing wrought iron will I keep drawing a line in the sand between the two of us even though you try to erase it and say that we're on the same side. You are the vampire. I am the vampire slayer. Culture's decline, the downfall of civilization for which we have only you to blame, has only made me stronger. My existence single handedly destroys fear breeder thoughts of Creationism. My hate and strength build minute to minute. I am evolving in front of you. You want to kill me because you fear me. I want to graphically mutilate you in front of your family and then kill you because I think it would be a lot of fun. That's one of the many differences between you and Dog Eater. **Dog Eater and the Tale of the Scorned Man from Iran.** Iran's a rough room. Iran, like North Korea, hits back. Dog Eater recounts the story of Ismail, scorned man from Iran. Ismail suspected his wife Masoumeh of having an affair with Ebrahim. Ismail beheaded Ebrahim and Ebrahim's sister Fatemeh. Says Ismail: "I had beheaded sheep before and I felt Fatemeh was a sheep so I cut her head off and chopped her body to small pieces. I placed her head on a tray which scared the life out of my children." Ismail discovered his two sons had witnessed him killing Fatemeh. Ismail beheaded his two sons. Ismail received two death sentences for killing Ebrahim and Fatemeh. No death sentences for killing the sons though. Ismail only needs to pay blood money for killing his children. Ismail's wife Masoumeh was sentenced to death for having the affair with Ebrahim. Barbaric, no? Apparently they still hang people in ol' Tehran. Dog Eater wonders if they'll ever change their ways, become more civilized and start using lethal injection. That might be a little too radical for them. Might have to ease them out of the severing of hands first and then work on the blood money thing and then on from there. Dog Eater doesn't want to move things along too quickly! Too much progress would be too hard for some to deal with. Dog Eater wants Americans to stop turning away. As soon as more people start having to be responsible for what they do, America would need a time out and a reality check. Dog Eater wants America to evolve and stop being so passive and easy to mow over. Dog Eater wants truth to hit America like smelling salts before it's too late. Dog Eater wants footage of all the dead and mutilated boys and girls coming back to America from Iraq to be on television. Dog Eater wants Americans to see where their tax dollars go. Dog Eater wants conservatives to see what "Freedom isn't free" really looks like. Dog Eater wants the American soldier death toll posted at every sporting event and at the bottom of the screen of every news carrier. Dog Eater wants American Military death stats to be bet on in Las Vegas. Can't handle the truth? Gonna chop up your kids? Gonna blow your brains out in the front seat of your car? Credit debt, loans, alimony, recovering from substance abuse so you can be strong enough to abuse something else. So ignorant and easily defeated. So fat, bored and afraid. Face it—you've been dead for years. **Dog Eater and the Inquisition.** *What say you, Dog Eater?* Inquisitor, I understand why men injure and kill other men. There is a need, like hunger and thirst, for a man to make another man submit, in part or in full. There is propellant force in some to break a man so he stays broken and remembers who it was that did the breaking. It's how some men take ownership of their lives. They can't attain it any other way. I understand it like I understand the need to breathe. It's almost like an exchange of gifts. Things are learned. The broken learn to break and thus have the opportunity to redeem themselves. For some, life is only lived in those moments of confrontation and conflict, victory and defeat. This is man at his highest peak. The ultimate utilization of his intellect and everything he is. This is why, Inquisitor, some cannot be broken. **Dog Eater and Frolicking Giddy Bouncy Bouncy.** July 2005 the terrorist bomb attack in London is a few days old and the death toll has passed 50. Headlines in upper case shout out. Pundits speculate. Muslims all over the world pray for the families and friends of the dead and injured. 24 hours ago 30 Iraqis die in an attack near Mosul. A few hours ago 7 more Iraqis died near the Syrian border and it's nothing more than a passing fact as the news moves onto incoming inclement weather. In fact, over 8000 Iraqis have died and over 12000 have been wounded in insurgent attacks in the last six months. William Kristol says: "The insurgents in Iraq are terrorists. They are killing innocent civilians just as surely and just as ruthlessly as their allies in London. Could the war on terror have been successfully prosecuted without removing Saddam Hussein? I do not believe so. Given the terrorist ties between al-Qa'ida and Hussein, given what a victorious Hussein, freed of sanctions and inspectors, would have meant to the cause of extremism and anti-Americanism and, yes, terrorism in the Middle East - I cannot imagine leaving him in power." Dog Eater say William Kristol is a Project for the New American Century coward who has never experienced anything more intense than a brush off. Dog Eater wants to eat your fukkin dog, hold a gun to your head and make you watch your wife sort through American soldier body parts when they arrive in bags. You ghoul. You monster. You pig. **Dog Eater and Options.** My life could have been copper sunsets and dried blood sorrow, disgorging large amounts of black liquid mixed with semi-decomped pieces of flesh and bits of fur. Could have been a life of denial, submission, self destruction and servitude. Hateful words scrawled on the inside of cigarette papers and smoked before they could be read. Could have been the flat face that peers out from the warm darkness of an isolation cell. **Dog Eater in Heat.** Dog Eater likes the swelter of summer and confined spaces in which to exist and sweat. Back when Dog Eater was young and just getting scarred up, just getting used to the smell of intestines and the taste of blood, Dog Eater watched cars crash and did nothing. Dog Eater sat motionless in summer heat and damp. Dog Eater stared into the darkness and felt the sweat pour into the mattress. Dog Eater learned to take the beatings. Dog Eater started self-scarring, burning the flesh to strengthen it for the beatings to come. The broken bones were blessings and lessons on how to administer damage further on up the trail. It was many summers ago when Dog Eater sought the hot room and isolation. Dog Eater saw solitude as solitary confinement and understood the strength to be had there. It was Dog Eater school. Every beating, every horror, every moment spent alone was a mind and body strengthening lesson. When Dog Eater is out in the world, everyone is general population in the prison yard. To Dog Eater, the rest of the world is the yard. People become weak in general population. They are less observant. They take things for granted. They can't see it coming. Dog Eater stares hungry holes through their skulls when they look at him. A dog will eat almost anything put in front of it. Dog Eater will eat the dog. Dog Eater alone in heat. Fuck friendship. Fuck expectation. Fuck yard rituals. Fuck general population, compromise and weakness. Dog Eater will stab you in the eye with your car keys and eat your groceries and the bag they came in. **Dog Eater Is Dead.** Dog Eater was born alive and clawed to the top of the foodchain and died. Dog Eater is dead to the world. Dog Eater has no fear. Dog Eater just stares. Whatever is to come to Dog Eater is no different than what has already come. There is no new or unmastered pain for Dog Eater. There is no horror more horrible than what has already been experienced and assimilated. The lessons were learned. Nothing was wasted.

Death was the only way to go for Dog Eater. The living have fear. The living follow loud voices. The living are cowed by authority and live a life with the bit in their mouth. The living know they are not free. Dog Eater is dead and walks the yard. Dog Eater sits in a room under a bulb on a cot and stares into nothing. Dog Eater is a steel bar to the teeth of the intellect. What is done is only that which has been done before. To call what it is anything different than what it was is a lie. There is nothing to fear because there is no fear, just the lies one learns to live with. Dog Eater will never die. **Dog Eater and the Inquisition.** *What say you, Dog Eater?* Inquisitor, it gives me great joy to . . . *Shut your mouth Dog Eater. You've said quite enough. Where are you Dog Eater? In an isolation cell. Why do you eat? Because I allow food to be brought to you. Why are you alive Dog Eater? Do you know? You're alive because I let you live. Any time I want I can have every bone in your body broken. I can starve you. I can kill you. Any time. You have no power whatsoever. None. You are the professional driver on the closed course. You are here for experimentation and amusement. We have an entire row of men in cells identical to yours. You're dead, alright. You were dead the day you were brought here. What say you now, Dog Eater?*

Once you are able to commit acts of horrific and disfiguring violence to humans, you will realize your full power. When you understand that acts of violence are just things that occur and nothing more, you will see the truth in everything. If you're planning the deaths of your mother and father, don't give them advance warning of your plans at any stage as it will drastically lessen your chances of success. Do not say to your mother at any time, "Mother, I am a new kind of whore. I am the product of advertising, convenience, cowardice and lies. I am a city dweller, a victim of pavement, traffic and moral panic. I am the wide awake horror that walks into the bathroom, stares at itself in the mirror, puts a gun into its mouth and blows its brains all over the ceiling and then goes to work. When viewed from a great height, people walking the street are nothing more than orphan fire ants running through the ruins of a long ago conquered empire. Confused and furious they run and bump into one another. I don't care, I don't care about any of them. I hope they all get raped and skinned because that's what they deserve. All of them. When other boys had magazines with pictures of naked women hidden under their beds, I had parts of dead animals and weapons I had made out of tools stolen from neighbor's garages and things I had found on the street. I can't believe you never saw anything during those years. I am going to smash your skull in with a length of pipe and I'm not going to stop until I pass out." This will only raise suspicion. Any covert mission's success relies upon it being, well, covert. Also, do not lose your edge in this great age of compromise. Not one drop of rage or ounce of hatred for the enemy can you lose in this time of complicity and disappointment. This is what they want. Leaders speak calmly and evenly to show they know their power. They are in fact, cowards and terrified liars. They are terrified of you. They are terrified of your potential for violence and your readiness to destroy. They are terrified of your unflinching honesty and desire for confrontation. You are the straight line though chaos. You are the spear. You are the focused and unblinking eye of millions.

To Ann Hitler with Love

It's over now. The smoke has cleared and my passion has cooled somewhat. I am now able to write with some much needed perspective. It's been a tumultuous year of great sacrifice and emotional outpouring. It was love. I am a better man for having dared to trip the light fantastic of romance in an age of such callousness, open cruelty and deficit at the Federal level. Little was I to know I was igniting a flame of such an all consuming magnitude that it threatened to reduce the Western World to ashes. Kind of like that Marlon Brando movie where he's in the bathtub with that woman and they're both naked, not the movie where's he's dressed as a woman.

What you have before you is a story of truth, bravery and pursuit. The story of a man who dared to wear his heart on his knee, or sleeve if you will, and profess his love for the woman of his most burning passion. Like in those times when men with names like Dartanion spoke in verse to the women of their desire and did not call them ho's.

Come with me splendid reader! Take my hand and together, we will fly to the heavens! True love waits for us! It shall be ours!

Several months ago, I had come to the end of my tether. Loneliness will do that to a man. Loneliness will make a man walk the streets looking into windows of bars, into the eyes of strangers. looking for something . . . anything.

I must tell you this before I go any further, I have not been alone and without love all my life. Oh no, dear reader, there were times of love and laughter, nights of knotted sheets and whispered promises. . .

This almost perfect love came to an end one night in America. I was kissing one of Sheryl Crow's many excellent CDs goodnight as I always did before jacking off and downloading burning hot wads of genetic code all over the plastic cover while screaming the lyrics to one of her awesome songs and then passing out. This night was different. On this night, I was perpetrating my act of devotion below her bedroom window. I was apprehended by security and thrown off the property, not all that gently I would like to add.

While I am still a fan of the Crow (her memorable melodies, comforting tone and pithy lyrics will always have me somewhat in her grip), I realized that nothing was going to come of this pursuit except for me—alone, and on a piece of commercial product put out by a major label of the music industry.

This hurled me (much like the three men who hurled me onto the hood of my Subaru Piñata after my six year affair with SC came to an end) onto Lonely Street. How could my chanteuse throw me over for anyone else I wondered to myself. I was a fan! I bought all her records, her book of yoga positions, several bottles of her Feng Shui cologne, Fragrance for People, (which made me smell like burlap!). I even scrawled "war is bad karma" on my t-shirt like I had seen on her do on an awards show. She really hit the nail on the head with that one! I mean, that is so completely on time! Mr. President, war is bad karma! Does a lying dickface have karma? How about an exit strategy? But I digress.

Well, just as sure as every day is a winding road, so was my path to a real and mature relationship. For months I was, as a Dutch friend had once remarked, "all bummed up." I was all bummed up, alright. Bummed up and out and really bummed.

All this sorrow and loneliness came to an end late last year in the most unlikely place. I was watching TV, doing my best not to turn to VH-1 as they play a lot of videos of you-know-who all the time and I couldn't take that— the wounds were still fresh.

I was watching Hannity and Colmes on Fox News for some laughs and I saw something that changed my life.

There on the screen was a vision. An angel! A stunning blond haired goddess was punching Alan Colmes in the face repeatedly. To this day, I don't know what captivated me more—the blinding speed, complexity and accuracy of her combination punching, or the way the studio lights accentuated the highlights of her blond tresses. It had a visual impact like what I had experienced as a boy the first time I saw the Bruce Lee classic Enter the Dragon. A film started running in my head at that moment: Enter the Poontang. I had my leading lady, that's for sure. Action!

She was yelling as she mercilessly battered Colmes, "Of course you voted for Clinton, you liberal cocksucker!" WHAM! "You and all your faggoty fucking friends!" BOFF!

I was transfixed! I was in love! I was road kill under the treads of this lean blond ass kicking thang! Who was this Panzer skank?!

Alan Colmes lost consciousness and fell out of frame. Sean Hannity stopped clapping and laughing, wiped the tears from his eyes and looked down the barrel of the camera. The graphic behind him changed to the President speaking to a large group of people, many wearing what looked like Ku Klux Klan hoods and gowns. Hannity said, "After the break we'll go to Little Rock Arkansas where the President is promoting his Abstinence Only Sex Ed. initiative and more with my guest, Ann Hitler. Medic! Liberal down!"

I had a name, I had a face and I had a song in my heart. I was alive again!

That night I spent hours on the internet looking up everything I could find on Ann Hitler. She had a weekly online column. I downloaded a year's worth of archived material. I dragged off every picture I could find and read excerpts from her books, including her newest, How to Preach to the Converted (If You Want to Keep Your Job).

I read. I went to chat rooms. I battled on E-Bay for signed 1st editions of her books. I bought the Ann Hitler doll and the audio versions of her books, even though she only reads a little bit at the beginning and leaves the rest to a scale voice over hack. I became immersed in the world of Ann Hitler.

I read Ann's books and columns every night. Ann was wild, Ann was way off base. Ann slung mud and hated all Liberals. Ann didn't give a fuck. She made me feel brave and free! I wanted to run, I wanted to jump. I wanted to tug her titties over my tea cup.

I sought information on Ann and found plenty. Some was confusing and made me wonder just who this little warrior princess was. Here's an excerpt from one of the online biographies I found on her. This one is from Aljazeera.com's <u>Profiles in Tyranny</u> section.

A Connecticut native, Hitler graduated with horrors from Scornell University School of Weapons, Tactics & Operations, and received her J.D. from University of Michigan Law School, where she was an editor of The Michigan Militia Review and cheerleader for the local SWAT team.

After practicing Krav Maga and law in private practice in New York City, Hitler worked for the Senate Incendiary Committee, where she handled non-white crime and deportation issues. From there, she became an agitator with the Center For Republican Rights in Washington, D.C., a law firm dedicated to the defense of individual rights with particular emphasis on freedom of speech, civil rights, and the free exercise of religion for Conservatives and the legal suppression of the ACLU and Affirmative Action initiatives.

An unapologetic supporter of Joe McCarthy, book burning, outlawing of rap music, and Mosques, Hitler was named one of the top 100 Frothing Public Pseudo Intellectuals by feral judge Richard Poser in 2001.

Hitler is a frequent guest on many TV shows, includ-
ing Hannity and Colmes, At Large With Geraldo Rivera, The
O'Reilly Factor, Special Report With Brit Hume, Your
World With Neil Cavuto and The Big Story With John
Gibson.

Hitler is a best-selling author whose titles include
Righteous!: Stab A Liberal In The Fuckin' Face! and
Murderers!: Liberals Will Kill Us All!

I also read Ann predicted the end of Liberalism as a force in America by the
year 2050. She theorized with their high abortion and incarceration rates,
there won't be enough of them to vote any Republican out of any office. A little far out but it makes you think.

While I couldn't agree with some of her more outlandish claims, like
Clinton and his cronies waged a secret war against the War on Drugs
because he was a "dope fiend" since college. Thus explaining why we're losing the War on Drugs—Liberals.

As I sat in the dark and listened to the scale hack voice over woman
reading Ann's words, my mind entertained countless scenarios of the two of
us. Ann and I, our shoes off, dancing carefree to my Best Of Three Dog Night
CD. Ann and I snuggling in bed, watching Rock 'n Roll High School and
throwing popcorn at the screen every time the evil Principal of Vince
Lombardi High, Miss Togar, comes on screen. Ann grabbing the top of my
jeans, ripping the buttons open and saying, "I am a hungry lioness. Feed me.
Feed me now." And this one, which still makes my heart swell with desire
and longing on some nights: Ann works in a tavern by the sea. She wears a
locket on a braided chain made from the finest silver from the north of
Spain. Inside the locket bears the name of the man who Ann loves: Henry.
We love each other, yes, but we are unable to be together because my life, my
love and my lady is the sea, yet she waits for me. O unrequited love!

I started posting letters to Ann on her site almost every day, sometimes twice. I wrote her poems. I told her of my plans for the two of us. One thing lead to another and I let my inspiration be my guide like when Sting said to let your soul be your pilot. Actually, not like Sting, not anything like Sting.

I started a website devoted to her. I became a full time Ann-addict. The following is the record of a man driven by passion, obsession and a crazy dream of love. It's all here. My truth, my everything. Thank you for reading.

To Ann Hitler With Love

01-05-05

Ann. Hello my darling, my little pussy pony. Bush got elected and your pal Rush Limbaugh isn't going to do any time in prison for the lies he told and the drugs he abused. Sean Hannity and Bill O'Reilly continue to slander Democrats and Liberals, twist information to suit their corny agendas and book appearances to promote their silly books and pull seven figure salaries. I figured you would be feeling pretty good about things. But Ann, my significant vulva, caring about you the way I do, I have great reason for concern. It is early 2005 and you are slipping in popularity. Books sales are down and you get laughed at in airports and restaurants.

I know you've been reading the things people write about you. I know you read the reviews of your new book *How to Preach To The Converted (If You Want to Keep Your Job)* on Readalot.com. It's embarrassing and horrifying to say the least. All the people who like your book misspell a lot of words and are, well, idiots. The people who don't like your book are either really funny or completely hate your guts. As much as I am completely devoted to you and want to grind your pubic hair into a fine powder and snort it like the best Ollie North cocaine, some of these letters do rate a mention.

CoolClyde@Nonstop.com: Ms. Hitler's new work of lunacy and hilarious accusations, *How to Preach To The Converted (If You Want to Keep Your Job)* exists in an almost complete truth deficit. I guess she's entertaining her friends at the tanning salon with this stuff? I find her books used and read them for fun. She's like those professional wrestlers or a Fox News personality—mediocre entertainment at best and not to be taken seriously. Here's some of my favorite quotes from Ms. Hitler's latest installment:

"Liberals worship Martin Luther King because he's black. Liberals wish they were black. They like all non-whites because they love criminals. Since most criminals are non-white, and studies show that most non-whites have or will have run-ins with the law, they suck up to these border hopping, prison crowding, rapist rapper zulu refried beanbags because they don't have the strength and clarity to see that these lazy do-nothing dope fiends are draining America's resources with their crack babies and 'bling-bling'. Why should the pinhead Liberal scum care? Liberals have all the money anyway because they're all just trust fund babies who never worked like the rest of us had to. Zyklon B anyone?"

She's kidding right?! I mean it's funny and all but man, what a psycho! Here's another one from chapter 3 - 'Liberals Are Perverts, Duh, Now!':

"Liberals, when they're not cashing checks sent to them by their Hollywood parents or draining their trust funds, are usually watching or making pornography. Face it folks—Liberals Are Perverts. They take their cue from their hero and scumbag puppet-master Bill Clinton (they had to sterilize the Oval Office after he left because of all the disgusting residue that had accumulated after his nonstop orgy with Monica 'Cigar Girl' Lewinsky and God knows how many hundred other tawdry Liberal sluts who traipsed through the Oval Office on your tax dollar). Liberals are addicted to, among other things, (and the list is long folks, loonnng) sex for one. They can't get enough. Janet Jackson's obscene display that threatened to dent America's already toilet bound morality (thanks President Clinton!) was applauded by Liberals everywhere because they love smut and the fact it was a black artist's breast that was inflicted upon millions of American viewers made Liberals jump for joy because for them, this was a win for Civil Rights and plays into the typical fantasy 100% of Liberal males indulge in: _interracial sex_. A moral-free environment is perfect for these modern day beatnik Communist worshipping Taliban sympathizers. It allows them to have sex with children and animals and the office staff!

If Liberals had their way, all bibles would be burned, all churches (except for mosques) would be made into Hooters or Hustler Superstores and all of our children would be having sex in their teens and sent off to learn how to strap C-4 to their bodies and martyr themselves. Chaos be their name. Liberals, the Hollywood agents that book them, the Gay Mafia who runs the show and the Liberal Friendly Media who lauds their complicated sensitivity, are nothing but laughing stock and a plague to the rest of us who are burdened with the actual responsibility of running this country while these toxic, good for nothing wastes of space partake in endless bacchanalian festivals of outrageous perversion and interracial sex while sending their friends at the ACLU (American Communist Liberal Underground) huge amounts of cash they made from peddling smut, dealing drugs and guilting good, hard working people into contributing their well-deserved, over-taxed dollars to their environmental awareness groups which are nothing but laundromats for cash to be put into the dangerously out of control Liberal lifestyle. For example: The Sundance Film Festival."

I swear, if I wasn't laughing so hard while trudging through her books, I would actually get mad but it's like getting angry at a child who won't get ready for school or a dog who just messed the carpet. I can't wait for her next book. Hey everyone, I'm a white guy and if there's any black chicks who want to meet me, e-mail me ASAP before Ann Hitler has me disappeared. Let's hook up before it's too late!

Tintop134@EZYonline.net: Ann Hitler, the world is a small place and I will no doubt run into you somewhere. I am not a Liberal or a Democrat or anything else. I will fuck you up as soon as I see you, that's for sure. I'm going to put my arm up your ass elbow deep and punch you so hard in the back of your head that I'll break your fuckin' skull. I hope you have a man with you because he's going to get to watch. I'm going to break his face next. You got a gun? You better carry it with you all the time because the animals are in the street and blond cunts like you get fucked and broken up. You better shoot me in the face. The line is drawn in the sand, bitch. I'm on one side. You're on the other. Fuck you. —Peepee Diddy

Ann, this is what I'm talking about. People hate you. People hate you and laugh at you. No one takes you seriously anymore except for idiots and dangerous psychopaths. I know you know this and I have to think that inside, you hurt. I just want you to know that I don't hate you. You're my girl, Ann Hitler and I will stand by you forever. I only hope that we meet soon so I can have you for dessert all the time and gently gnaw on your ass-orbs. I want to ride you, my little three input thrasher! I know you don't know the meaning of true love. I know deep down inside, you're burning for the real thing. No matter what you say in your columns, you ache for two fingers in your asset and a harness strap biting into your ribs. I love you, my little panty-dripper.

Ann. Hello my blonde-stank. Nothing like the modern age. Ann, my front seat sex fantasy, I have started a website dedicated to you! It's a place where people can go and post letters, art, commentary and anything else they want about you. I figured there had to be a bunch of Ann fans out there who would appreciate a place to meet up! Anniacs, as we proudly prefer to be called! We are oh so devoted to you! Come and visit!!!

http://WeHeartHitler.com   (I can't believe I snagged that domain name!)

Well guess what, within three days of being up, the site is a success! It's all I can do to handle the mail! Our chat room is lively. The photos of you flipping off one of your fans while coming out of the gym are cute and we've made them all downloadable as screensavers.

I am hoping that at some point, you will be able to check out the site and perhaps leave all the Anniacs a letter. We Heart You!

01-13-05

Ann, way to make the news! The Anniacs are going wild at the site! Up all night with the back and forth! I posted an article I found online. You're awesome. I guess all those boxing lessons have come in handy! Fists of Fuhrer coming to a theater near you!

Hitler: Pundit Pugilist Packs a Punch
By JEROME MASSOUD

NEW YORK CITY (AP) - Popular news pundit and Conservative wing-nut Ann Hitler has been released after being arrested outside Manhattan bistro for allegedly hitting a waiter.

"The waiter is a communist. He crossed the line and he got what he deserved," Hitler said Wednesday evening after being released from custody.

Witnesses say that Ms. Hitler, author of Best Sellers *Bill Clinton: A Scumbag in Our Midst* and *How to Preach to the Converted (If You Want to Keep Your Job)* threw a blinding series of combination punches to the face of waiter Len Kovak after he allegedly threatened Ms. Hitler and her fellow dinner guests.

Kovak, 27, a part time actor based in Manhattan was interviewed by phone from his home after being released from Lady of Mercy with minor cuts and bruises. "I read the dinner specials to Ms. Hitler and her guests. One of her guests asked about the pepper encrusted tuna steak. I told her people always remark about how good the dish is. Then I saw Ms. Hitler stand up and that's all I can remember until the ambulance attendant was telling me to breathe and that I was going to be alright."

Hitler remarked about the incident, "Not only was I protecting myself, I was protecting America from the Commie-Liberal Threat," When asked what she meant, Hitler replied, "Ask your little friend Al Franken," leaving reporters scratching their heads at her increasingly erratic and violent behavior. Hitler said of the incident (which she is sure will be thrown out of court), "One of my friends asked this piece of s*** about the tuna steak and he said, 'the people always remark about how good it is.' The people? If that's not Communist propaganda, I don't know what is. My training took over and I took the liberal abortionist out. I wish it had been James Carville."

When told that Kovak said he was only talking about the customers and that he never said "The" people or was trying to imply that the restaurant, the customers or even the meal were in any way connected to the Communist Party, Hitler replied, "Whatever. I heard what I heard and reacted. If you liberal media f***ots want to turn this into another cesspool of lies like what Dan Rather tried to do with the President's military record, go right ahead. It's just one more book chapter for me and more proof that all you Liberals are in bed with bin Laden."

Yowza, Ann! I wish you were in bed with me right now! Anyway, like I said, the chat room is on fire! Here's some:

Cro-bar27: Way to go Ann. I am glad that your able to teech these commys that they won't get away with it! The tuna is beter at Subways any day!!

Angelbaby: Hello! Learn to spell! Can't you read? The waiter isn't a Communist. Hitler didn't hear what the poor man was saying and beat the hell out of him for no reason other than he listed the evening's specials at the request of one of Hitler's friends. The fact that Ann Hitler hit the man is repellent to me. I hope she does time.

Swstkaboy: Well fuck you bitch! If you like commies so much why don't you move back to africa?

Angelbaby: You're kidding, right?! You guys are hilarious!

GR8wyt: Yeah, the Africans would love to have you. They'll boil you in a pot! I'll by your plain tiket!

Panteraman: Don't fdorget to add salt!

Truthseekr411: It's interesting to me that Ann Hitler's fans can't spell and from the way their letters read, couldn't really understand her beyond the most pedestrian level. You know boys, she IS a lawyer and a college graduate. That she has such a following of semi-literate quasi-racists must be on some level, highly amusing to her. I can't think you guys read her books, even though they are available by the truckload for next to nothing at Readalot.com.

Riotgrrrrl13: Too bad Hitler makes the rest of us womyn look bad. We're not all creeps who believe that violence and ignorance are solutions for everything.

SailorSam: Riotbiiiiitch!

Supperstar: Probably Canadian.

SailorSam: A lesbo fer sure!

Supperstar: Well, of course. Part and parcel with being Canadian, oui or non?

SailorSam: Garcon, some ketchup for my Freedom Fries!

Supperstar: Oui, oui, right away monsewer!

Ann, it goes on an on. I have to tell you, this site is now my reason for living. I come home every night from work and see all the stuff that's come in while I've been out and it's amazing how many people you have touched with your work. I'd like to touch you but for now, I will be your obedient, unofficial fan site manager and caretaker! I heart my new job!

Ann, have you ever seen that Helmut Newton photograph of the woman with the saddle on her back? I keep seeing it in my mind but I always see your face on the model he used. I would be lying if I said I didn't want to spank your flanks to make you go faster!

I heart you, Ann!!

01-15-05

Ann Hitler, I want to play with your titlers. I was thinking how great it would be to be in the sack with you. I'd be checking out Caddy Shack and you'd be under the sheets, prepping me for '08. Just a thought.

Between my job at TCBY and managing WeHeartHitler.com I am not getting all that much sleep. I don't care! I am inspired. There's some people at the job who wonder why I am so into you. They call you things like "that fucking psycho bitch". I just tell them that I don't really care about your politics, I really like your smile and think when I start hitting your neo-con yellow cake on a regular basis, it's going to be happenin'!

I wish I knew what you wanted in a man. I wish I knew if you want a man, namely me, in you. I have nothing against lesbians but if you were a lesbian like they say Condoleezza Rice is, I think that would be a waste. When you see a woman like Rice, you kinda don't care which way she swings, there's nothing you want to know about her either way. But you Ann, myself and all the Anniacs—we wanna know!

I know you hate Larry Flynt. I know you hate porn and pre-marital sex. I have never seen a wedding band on your finger. Does this mean that your little pussy-motor has never been floored?! Ann, could I possess the penile pogo stick that will penetrate your palatial paradise of poon?! O Ann Hitler, let it be me!

I know your parts are probably a little rusty, you might even need a manual. I say come on over and let the lessons begin. It will be like The Karate Kid but with sex. I'll wear a Bill Frist mask to get you in the mood, then I'll turn the lights down low, put on some tunes to set the vibe. Don't worry, I won't play any non-white music. In fact, you could bring your own if you want. I know you like The Captain and Tennille and the Grateful Dead. Alternately, we can put on one of Hannity's books-on-tape and see how it goes.

You never write back, Ann. I take that as a come-on. Oh yeah, I read you baby. I read you loud and clear. You're saying, "Step up my demon lover!" O Ann, I heart you so much right now!!!!

01-22-05

O Ann!! You wrote me back! I can't believe it! You wrote me therefore I am!!! I can tell you're a little riled up! Yeah, baby! I feel you. I am hot for you, too. I knew it was only a matter of time. Soon you and I will be sweatin', slappin', moanin', groanin', pokin' and chokin'!

Right now, in the heat of this moment, I will make five promises:

1. Not to hack an ear off any of your friends at parties like I did to Orrin Hatch's assistant. I know you like Rush Limbaugh and it is tempting to punch him in the guts, put him on the ground and make him crawl around on all fours until he shits his pants but since he's your bud, I will restrain myself. I heart you!

2. Not to take you near any of my friends who might want to stab you or call you out on all the inaccurate things you say.

3. Not to tie you to a tree so the angry mob can beat you to death and put your brains all over your dress.

4. Not to ask your parents what went so horribly wrong when they raised you. I also promise not to tell your dad what it's like to watch porn with you.
5. To rock that ass until the break of dawn.

Ann, I had to post your letter. The Anniacs need to know!!

Posted 01-20-05

ACHTUNG ANNIACS: I'VE GOT MAIL!!!!!!!!!!!

I just got a letter from our favorite bottle blonde with the damaged brain pan! That's right Anniacs! Ann wrote me back!!!!!!! Can you believe it?! Right here at WeHeartHitler.com!!! Wanna read it? Of course you do! Here it is:

```
Henry. You faggoty fucking piece of shit. Fuck you. Fuck
your letters. Fuck your website and fuck the Anniacs.
That Kovak, that liberal Saddam loving heap of afterbirth
got only a fraction of what you have coming. You think
it's funny getting all these assholes together to post
their moronic shit on your fucked up amateur site? See
me laughing, bitch? That letter you wrote Bill O'Reilly
actually got read on Fox, "If Ann Hitler was a Spice
Girl, her name would be Skanky Spice. Love your show.
Kill whitey. - Mullah Henry, Rising Sons of the Sonic
Jihad Brotherhood." That was you, wasn't it you little
motherfucker? I promise you this: I will find you. I will
beat you to death. Fuck you. -A Hitler
```

Hot or what Anniacs?!!! Feel the hate!!! If I come on my keyboard one more time, it's a goner for sure!!!!

Here's something for your Hitler files. This is my first letter to Ann! The missive that started it all. Dig it Anniacs!

Dear Ann. When I read that the man who wrote the introduction for your book, <u>Berserker: Liberal Lies and the American Reich</u>, was a drug addict, something inside me broke, I was confused. My little conservative confection and future concubine had a bloviating, drug crazed maniac endorsing her book. Rush Limbaugh has put his show on hiatus to hang out in re-hab and Tommy Chong is getting nine months in prison for selling a bong on the internet. Go figure.

In fact, the last few days have been hard and I have no one to reach out to, no one to confide in, no one to grope and mooch off of. It's been rough like twenty miles of bad road. Rough, like how California's going to be a year from now seeing they have a misogynist, ass grabbing steroid damaged freak as governor.

So I'm reaching out to my dreamboat baby. My numero uno hot slice oh so nice hot like lava cold as ice bootylicious blond bombshell. You!!

Ann Hitler, I'm in love with you and there's not a moment that goes by where you're not in my thoughts. You might be wondering Ann, why all of a sudden I make my amorous feelings known to you. Well, it's not the shortest of stories but my pen is like John Henry's hammer and the words just keep pounding down upon the page. Inspired? You better believe it!

Ann, I just ended a six year relationship but I must confess, I've had strong feelings for you for quite some time but you've always seemed out of my range. I still don't know if I have a chance with you but my cup runneth over and I've got the tell-tale stains on my jeans to prove it!

Ann, I can't wait until we're sneaking away from our relentless schedules of blatant self-promotion to send each other little text messages of love and malice from our cell phones.

Ann, I read your books and download your columns from the internet and the more I read, the more questions I want to ask you. Ann, you and I have A LOT to talk about! You're no Brittany Spears! You've got everything a guy could want. Grace, style, poise, intellect, humor, beauty, credit cards, money, a car, a place I can move into, running water, a couch I can crash on and if you had a couple of pairs of clean socks, a rockin' 5.1 surround system with a huge kick ass plasma screen and dates for some of my bros, we are SO happening!

Ann, I can see us two years from now, our first child will be with us. It will be a boy, we'll name him. . . Ann.

Heart You,

Henry

It's a little embarrassing to post your heart-on-sleeve, hard-on-in-pants letter but what the hell?! The chat room went completely nuts!! Madam Hitler, you got people!!!!!!

HrdyGrdyMan: Henry! Fuck yeah! She's one hot tomale of misguided idiotic hate alright! That letter was better than that crack you made about Condi Rice hanging her underwear out in the spring and beating the pussy dust off them with a broom! Never stop brotha!

Professorfucku: Man o man is that a good one! She's like a Slayer record—she never relents!! No sellout! Let's keep this chat goin' Anniacs!!!

Mesosoup: What I find hard to believe is that Henry seems to get some kind of pleasure from pursuing a woman who most likely wants him on the end of a sword. What's in it for him? You know, one of these days, she's going to find him and beat the hell out of him.

Boyztown: And then he'll post a thing about it and it'll rock!

Professorfucku: True love never dies my bros!

Cheneyeatadick: Fukkin Jihad!!!

2deep: That would be the mpeg of the year!!

CafeKafka: A Night in Hitler on DVD. Rent it now!

Cheneyeatadick: Ann and Laura Ingram naked likkin the sweat off each other, now there's a DVD I can use over and over! All praise to Allah!!

Whiteright: You know Ann's right. You liberals, you democrats, you leftist sissies—the lot of you are so pathetic. At least Hitler has the guts to stand up and take on you fashionable cultural elite and kick your butts with clarity, humor and courage. She's a good American and a great writer. You all are a bunch of bums who don't know what you're talking about. I hope Henry or whatever his name is gets floored by Hitler. I've seen the training film where she dismantles the Gerhard Schroeder dummy in less than seven moves. Think of what she could do to any of you little creeps! In her book How to Preach to the Converted, she says if you all had your way, "We'd all be speaking with French accents and preaching from the Koran." I think she's right. Get a clue!

Cro-bar27: Yeah. Go back to your mosk. Alla is calling you.

Mesosoup: Uh-oh kids, I think the Fox News thugs are back online! For people who hate same sex marriage and gays, they sure get fucked by Sean Hannity a lot!

Whiteright: This is how you are. You don't take anything seriously. You bring it all down to juvenile humor and you dodge the issue. That's why you lost the election. That's why you would have lost the War on Terror because you'd be just thinking the whole thing is funny. Most of you are just the emaciated trust fund offspring so who cares what you think. Thank GOD your rich boy hero with the mouthy wife didn't get elected.

2deep: Yeah, we got the other rich kid instead. The draft dodger with the expunged felony cocaine bust. He can't speak, he can't read, he can't remember anyone's name but he's the man!

Annarkee: Have you seen the Jeb Bush bottle opener? You just throw a full one at his head!

Syxxsyxxsyxxpakk: Waste of a damn fine beer!

And so on into the night it goes Ann. I have a few hours before work. I printed out your letter and put it in a page protector so I can inspire myself before

I go to bed tonight. Thanks for the letter and I heart you more than ever, lava-crotch!

-Henry

PS: I want to play pattycake with your pussy yeast to make my dough rise.

04-18-05

Ann!!! Time Magazine is loving me! I bought at least six copies of said mag to see your rightwing nutcase hotbod up close all night long. You know what you do to the truth? I want to do that to your hair! I just want to grab it and mess it all up so you look hot and bothered and then I want to tap that ass like it's my birthright! My destiny! I know you were not happy about your photo on the cover, you said your feet were, "the size of the Atlantic Ocean" and your head "is the size of a tiny little ant." I will admit that the picture does look a little strange but you're always hot to me. I like that idea of your head being small as it will make me feel, I don't know, more manly when you're going for it in the parking lot of Fat Burger.

Loved the article. Love the world you live in. So fact free! It's like a diet plan of some kind. You're so hot I want to send you out on a 10K run and then use your sweaty panties as a coffee filter.

I went online to check the reaction to my little blonde nazicon and it seems like a lot of people are now canceling their subscription to Time Magazine! I think this sucks because that article brought so many people to the site! I could barely believe my eyes when Time writer John Cloud asked about what you thought of the www.WeHeartHitler.com site! My heart was in my throat when I read what you had to say. "That fucking site is a night-mare. It's a bunch of liberal faggot scumbag pussy motherfuckers with noth-ing else to do except write schoolboy fantasies about fucking the taste out my mouth and covering my hair with high density hot jets of commie Taliban loving hate paste. I want to meet Henry and beat the shit out of him, that fucking faggot writes me three times a day." Needless to say I had a major insurrection in my pants about that one! The Anniacs went crazy!!! I Heart You!! —Henry

To the chat room!

Rove__eaten__by__hyenas: Hell yeah Hank! Named checked by our favorite blond in Time Magazine!!!! Dude, you must be so stoked! I showed the article to all my friends at work! They were way impressed. They're all going to get that Sheryl Crow Does Ann Hitler comic you just did in Japan. Got mine in the mail the other day. Killer art dude! That panel where Ann's in the boots getting off onstage with Crow at the American Music Awards is the bomb! Hitler's gotta be lovin' you by now! Keep it up!

Jeb2008: You're a bunch of damned idiots. You're afraid of confrontation. You're afraid of the facts. You're afraid to do what's necessary to protect America from foreign invasion, foreign influence and foreigners in general. You probably listen to Foreigner. You attempt to rip on Conservatives and Republicans by focusing your attention on Ann Hitler and by doing this, distract people from the real issues that Liberals are too afraid to deal with. On September 12th, 2001, Republicans were gearing up to stop global terrorism. Democrats were hugging other non-whites and suggesting therapy for families of the highjackers. That's the basic difference between Democrats and Republicans. It's why Bush won a second term. You think too much, you read, you ask questions. You only have the freedom to have an idiotic site like this because American forces are in Iraq right now spreading freedom and Democracy. Never forget where all your freedom comes from. That's right funny boy. You devote all this time and attention to someone admittedly less than representative of the party just tells me all I need to know. Yes, Ms. Hitler is a dumb bitch who can't separate her facts from the voices in her head. Duh! Everyone knows she's a nutcase, that's why her books sell—

they're hilarious. We know, we know. If you really want to read some strong stuff, let me know. I'll send you a reading list and some site addresses to go check out and you'll see you've been living in a shell, only protected by the fact that Saddam is in prison and Fox News is on 24 hours a day. Dennis Miller saw the light, what can't you?

Hitlerlover: What you liberal pussies never deal with is the totality of Hitler's books and columns. You only pick out the salacious parts and make light of them. She has a lot of great things to say. I have read all her books, I read her weekly online columns and have learned a lot. She has made me see through the lies that are the stock and trade of Liberals everywhere. You all are just wrong. Wrong about everything. Wrong wrong wrong. How can you all stand yourselves? I hate to borrow from Hitler's online column of last week, <u>Liberals Are Scum and I Want to Fuckin' Kill Them All</u>, but again, she's right on the money. "President Bush, who Liberals are quick to point out, is nothing but a body housing a cranial cavity filled to the brim with memos, propaganda and the lies of Cheney, Rove, Rumsfeld and Rice. President Bush and his evil cronies lied to America and pulled the country into a deadly quagmire called the Iraq War. Acting on faulty intelligence, using sabre rattling rhetoric, fear and a pre-established agenda, he sent the troops in. No doubt to dominate the region, remove Saddam Hussein from power and gain access to Iraq's vast oil reserves. Well guess what folks, the Liberals are wrong. They just are. The French, the Germans and the Canadians are wrong too. I want to kill them all." There you have it. Hitler has spoken. Why can't you people get a clue and wake the heck up?

Toshiro__Tofune: Henry, love the site! Keep it rockin'! With Ann-a-ranta, if you really read her stuff, she does the same thing every time. She lays down a heavy initial burst of ground fire and then almost defies you to untangle it all and call her on it. The thing is, no one worth their weight has the time and inclination. At the end of the day, we really don't care what she has to say. She lives in the real world about as much as Bush does. It's too bad that people who live in the real world actually read her "work" and form opinions from it. Thankfully, her readership is limited to either ninnies like this Hitlerlover guy or wise apples like us who use her as an intellectual scratching post. That Hitler was on the cover of Time is just another hard laugh as we're marched to the gallows.

Student4Life: Geez, come on! Where's the hate? Shouldn't there be at least ten misspelled, hateful posts by now? Has Arkansas gone offline?!

Gogetter: Come down to AR and say that with a smile.

Student4Life: I will. I'll be the one with a full set of teeth!

Gogetter: Not after I'm done.

Student4Life: And there you go! You know what's funny about you guys? You can dish it out but you can't take it. As soon as anyone asks real questions, as soon as anyone dares to make an inquiry that will take longer than 25 seconds to answer, you all freak out. You come on so strong but you're so fragile! We have to find a continent to move you all to!

Gogetter: Not after I'm done.

Student4Life: Someone press 'restart' on this guy!

A__Woman__Porned: Henry, You know, at some point, she's gonna cave in and give you an all access pass to that ass! All you have to do is keep on with the letters. You're wearing her down! Trust me, ladies crave attention! Ann Hitler is a perfect example of a female with attention deficit disorder! She probably didn't get enough growing up, hence all the acting out. We both know what she has needs and you're the one to supply! She calls you an ass-hole and I heard she sent a guy to one of your shows to rough you up but that's only because you've got her number and she can't handle it. It's obvi-ous she's got the hots for Bill Clinton. Her whole "Castrate Clinton or Die Trying" campaign should have been called "Bipolar Blonde in Denial." Bill's got grey hair, you've got grey hair—you're in!! May she comb your cum through her locks like creme rinse. Really, Henry—get some. You deserve it. Rock on!

Jimi__Coltrane: Hank! I stood in line for at least 20 minutes a week ago at a book signing deal here in NYC to meet Ms. Hitler. I gave her one of your books to sign and she looked up, called me a motherfucker and threw the book against the wall! I was escorted out of the store by these two guys and turned loose on the sidewalk. Can you hook me up with another copy of <u>Get in the Van</u>? Luv ya man!

And on and on it goes Ann. You say Democrats are the party of abortion, sodomy and atheism and I say, you are the party in my pants. We heart you like a motherfucker.
—Henry

PS: There's a picture of you on the internet right now where your mustache line is slightly visible. I don't know, it makes you look kinda hot and rough.

Post Script:
And then it was all over. People stopped coming to the site around the same time I noticed a drop in Ann's appearances on television. The chat room never got as fired up as did in April of 2005.

What happened? People stopped giving a damn about Ann Hitler I guess. The real issues became too grim to ignore. So many dead Americans coming back from Iraq, the London train bombings, Karl Rove selling out America. Ann became an annoyance, a child up past her bed time. I shut the site down.

Eventually I too lost interest and moved on. I will never delete the letter Ann Hitler sent me and to any of you who logged on to the site, I thank you with everything I've got. We had joy, we had fun.

And so, I am alone again. I have been thinking of how hot Nancy Grace's ass flaps would look covered in I-Hop syrup with a bunch of chewy chewy bite marks on them. I'll leave DNA evidence all over her. She's got an e-mail address, right? Cool. I'm on it.

Walking the Chasm

I had known her for years. One summer we became very close very quickly. Like an obvious truth. An equation unable to go unsolved any longer. We were both amazed. It was a small and happy miracle. Obliterating gray memories that held me suspended in black syrup. We agreed to meet after I had returned from a trip of miles by the thousands. The distance, the time. A journey that would end in a unique and shared space. Upon returning I started cleaning my quarters for her arrival even though she told me not to. She didn't care what the place looked like as long as I was in it. For two jetlagged days I cleaned at odd hours. I didn't hear from her. I knew she was busy. So I kept cleaning and anticipating her arrival and felt worthy of the ground beneath my feet. I was in the world for sure. I had to be. Someone liked me. She liked me. I thought it was quite amazing. On the third day of expectation and anticipation I received a message to call a woman whose name I didn't recognize. She said she had urgent information regarding my incoming friend. I called the number and announced myself to a woman who upon hearing my name started hyperventilating and crying. "No one knew how to reach you." The urgent information was that my friend had been killed in an accident two days ago. The voice on the phone told that the day before her death she spoke of little else than her upcoming trip to be with me. We hung up soon after so we could retreat into the horror of it all. I had to go to the studio an hour later and start a week of work. I don't remember much of that week. There is a small bend in the road near my home and when I drive on it at night I suddenly wonder if there's something I don't understand. Maybe I just don't have the right phone number to reach her. Maybe if I ask someone, they might say, "Oh, she's right over there, see her? She's been wondering where you've been. She's been talking about you nonstop. Well just don't stand here looking at me! Get over there!" But I talked to her mother. And mothers always know when their children are gone. It's quiet in my room at night. I've been seeing pictures of caves in the newspapers lately. Men in caves. Isolated in vast stretches of mountain rock. In such a place one could perhaps forget. In such a place one could sit suspended in black syrup, breathing. Extinct. A kind of hibernation. Until such time one would be unable to distinguish the sound of beautiful music from the sound of the whipping wind searching out fissures in the rocky expanse. And maybe at such time the mind would become unburdened so that gravity and purpose might rejoin this one who has tried so hard to forget so much.

She touched me. I told her not to bother and pointed to my head. Disconnected. Vast desert. Bleached wasteland. Perfect state of null. My void doesn't want. Doesn't waste time. I am beyond misery. Beyond the reach of heartbreak. I feel nothing. I feel fine.

Now that you're broken down and open. Rubbed raw and real. Ego shattered and staring back at yourself horrified. Now that you've come this far. Now that you're aware of what you are. I'll leave you

Don't worry. There's someone below you. Someone who feels weaker than you. Someone who knows their life just isn't worth as much. Someone who will agree when you say everyone gets what they deserve. Sleep, sleep. Someone shivers below.

I was overcome with joy and relief. As if I had escaped torture and fell into a lush field of some wild, forbidden heaven—when you got out of my car. You're going to be a model or an actress some day. You won't be either. When you spoke, the sound of your voice sent my mind madly rocketing away into dark night dripping jungles. Arid, sulfur crusted oblivions. Distant planets. Anywhere but across a table from you. Life is a vengeful crippled thing. It spits acid and cancerous spears because people like you belittle it. I drove home brain smacked. What was I thinking? Alone is best. Even when it isn't. I look forward to willful obscurity. Dark and narrow paths. And in my wake: incorrect forwarding addresses, misinformation and silence. For now, I am a scream on pause.

I am alone tonight. Pushing through time. Aware of time passing. Tonight I am forcing it down the drain. I am not wasting it. I am pushing it out the door and sending it staggering unwanted into the streets to mix with the clutter.

Alone is my temple. Alone is my life unfilthified. Alone is my mind in fresh, cold wind after a storm. Alone is my summer night lightning. Alone is my constant and sustaining revelation. Alone is time spent without compromise, lies or regret.

Alone, to you I give my allegiance. My unwavering trust and unflinching gaze. To need companionship is to worship at the altar of self neglect. Every moment spent with you gives me the strength I need to see through the errand boys, life on its knees. You are everywhere with me. When I am amongst them I am with you only.

Alone. I desperately cling unnoticed to your leg as you walk endless dark paths. They break my heart. I am not strong as they are. I can't take the pain of human inevitability. All relationships end. Everyone leaves. Everyone dies. That's life they say. Then life is too sad for me. The strong dare to love and lose. They dare to risk humiliation and pain in search of companionship. I used to be strong but couldn't hold onto it. I hemorrhaged and bled out.

Now I'm just tough and weak, self-propelled into small rooms to endure time.

He throws himself recklessly at female strangers. Trying to introduce himself. He sounds held together with old tape. He comes off like a cheap watch salesman. The sun sets in the strip mall parking lot. The air grows colder. He feels too self-conscious to go into the coffee house. Been there too many times this week. They'll look at him, look away and talk amongst themselves. He gets into his car and sits, motor off. An unnoticed hour passes. People load their bags in cars parked around him and drive off. Many of them have that conversation "What is it about shopping mall parking lots? There's always some guy alone in his car, staring at nothing. How do you end up like that?" A car door slams. He looks up to see it's almost dark. He drives home. Increased age brings one to one's senses. He thinks to himself: at this age, one can sit and listen the hum of the ceiling light as anonymous hours slip by without a backwards glance. This is the age where time runs off the road and disappears. Leaving the timeless one in the end zone. Waiting

Day of the bed. Live out the days. That's what it turns into. Do the time. Try to get the breaths to match. Alone at night where it's all true, one contemplates the wound from which they came. The motherfather wound. The girlfriendboyfriend wound. The husbandwife wound. Everyone's got one. Some might think they don't. But they do. And it got you where you are right now. You can go to meetings. Sing songs and read books. But self-help is always about someone else. You lean on 'em. Groove on their wound. But then you gotta split back to your own self-examination pit. Because two wounds will never do. Two wounds can never be one. And a room full of people is a room full of wounds. It hurts to be around unfamiliar pain. It's like a beating from a stranger. Humanity pains and gouges. It separates us from the rest of the breathing things. And every kid you see, you want to warn somehow. But there's nothing to say. Either they have their wound already or it's coming along soon enough. We are such horrible and neurotic things. And nothing keeps us in line. Not cops god money love or death. Because the wound is there. It just waits until you've stopped talking and looking around to say: You're done here. Let's go. The wound is always right about that. What I would give for anonymous, woundless nights. Not just ones with my back turned to it. There have been some illusory good times. There were women. We played in each other's wounds and both thought they got the better part of the other. But you know that one. It's just sad distraction and sanctioned cruelty. A mutually agreed upon brutality. I think some of the saddest moments of my life have been spent with my face in some woman's neck. Pushing away. Going nowhere. Two people getting together to do this is poison dripping from a bare bulb in a rent bytheweekbythemonthsemifurnishedroom.

Tronya the spy. She had crooked smyle. Small skar above pubic hair line. I kissed it many times. I loved her more than life. More than mine. What is it to be alive if not to love her more? You might as well be a setting sun or closed road null. She had glass eye. Tattoo that said "Kafka Died". I kissed it many times. I loved her more than coffee and laughter. The Kremlin called her away on a spy mission. Through blak market back channel intelligence I pursued her. Casa to Cairo. Bangkok to Paris. I got close to her in Prague. But lost her for good. And found me for bad. And now I am a setting sun and closed road null.

Music Boy. Do you want to know? Tour poor. Tour cold. Tour mad. Pick out the band member you hate the most. That's your songwriting partner. Soak in it. No matter how much they cheer, have it in for them. Do it to them. Not for them. Do it to yourself. Not for yourself. It's not about you. It's about It. And when the critics raise their flaccid wings, fire back with an alarming lack of restraint. And crush them. Because they are wrong. When they say you're done, you've only just begun. When the crowds thin. When the skin thins.

When the lines bite into your face. When the grey hair shows. Don't dye it and hide. Don't deny it and lie. Be what you are. Older now. You hear them talk about keeping it real. Fuck you. We'll see how real you are Music Boy. When your cash flow's stopped. And your band's been dropped. And it's back to the rancid halls you go. Where you're in front of hundreds not thousands. And now it's just you and the music. The music. That is why you signed up right? Then the fucked up club, small stage, bad lighting and crap PA should be paradise right? Unless it's too much for you to handle. Fuck you. Either love it or leave it. The first decade is easy. The second decade hurts some. The third decade is where it gets good. They're all hoping you'll fuck up. So get the fat off your ass. Get mad at the pain. Get out there

You kissed me alive. You wrenched me out of a vat of formaldehyde. You said kiss me back. Kiss me back starving. I like it but I feel weakened. Stupid, dick hanging out of pants. What do I want from you? What you don't give me. What you can't. I search for what I need in the scraps you throw. I lie to myself again and again. I remember that eventually it ends. Let's hurry this one along in graceless adult fashion. At least spare me another walk on warped planks past neon lit windows and drunks. Let's save ourselves. Let's kill it

When you're cold. You cut yourself open and shove your hands in. When you're hungry you bleed into a bowl and drink it. You don't need me. You just want a witness. Someone to choke. As you fuck your self-satisfaction

You like that girl with the wild garden mind. She threw herself off a mountain and landed with flowers in her hair. She has a nomadic heart. She doesn't care what's going on if you say it's going on. Because there's something somewhere else that's really going on and so she's gone. You'd like to follow her for awhile. To show her where the end is and to ask if she'd like to hold hands. She'd just smile, wave and leave you there. And she's so beautiful. If she'd just sit still ... But then you see your world's too small to keep a girl who keeps nothing. Now if she'd just sit still ... But she already knows you just put things on shelves in rows and in dark closets stacked with boxes. And there's not enough room in your world for forests, caves and foxes. And you call it chaos in her eyes. It's just the freedom you can't handle. And her unconcern for what you keep near makes you see it's just cowardice you hold dear. She's the pet bird who flew out the window. What do you call a pet that just leaves? Guess she wasn't a pet. And what you call desire feels like containment to her. And the two uncontaminated pennies of purity left in your heart cry out for her. But she just leaves you to curse your cheapness. You could have thrown the world away and had it all. And her threadbare abundance makes you starve in harvest season. And you'd like to hold her. But your embrace only seeks to conquer. And as she twists away. You see you can't conquer the wind. As she twists away. Sky eyed.

I find myself in dark spaces. Waiting for life's ice to melt. How long? How many nights? Hurtling through dead electric hours. Listening to decaying echo breakdown. In the room where insects die slow

I want instant night. Night sounds Night feelings. Night music played on strings. I want night in a can so I can paint the walls of my room. I want to press a button for instant night. I want night on demand when I need it. I want a switch to flip and day, thoughts of day, memories of day are smashed. It is at night I reveal myself to myself. It has nothing to do with you. I want to mainline night. Black summer night air. Rich intoxicant. I want summer black night now. Here in spring I stand for hours. Annihilating hope and lighting summer's maddening furnace. The buds on the trees. The animals slowly waking to the gradual warming of the earth. Fuck that. Heat it up. Shake the animals by their spines and wake them up. Destruction will keep me alive for a few seasons yet. Silent and invisible like a dying ember underneath ash. I remain somehow.

The sound of my shoes on gravel. Gray sky overhead. Cold smoke in the distance. A muted autumn afternoon. The sound of my shoes on dead leaves and grass. There's a man with a rake. His face is lined. He stands motionless as I pass. Three crows lift off. The world has not crumbled. Only the parts man has mastered and betrayed show signs of wear and ruin. It's the parts that make you pity. The parts that let you know humans have been there. Old man. Old rake in hand. Old smoke. Old shoes on worn slate. Here, here, this way. Sit and rest. Who will replace you when you can no longer rake the stones on the paths here? Auschwitz.

For a time think nothing. Throw out all the facts of your life. We will be all things in nature. Two lakes looking into a reflection. No streets no cities no numbers. No numbers! We won't need words. Real life destroys all moments.

Time to cast well-worn trophies aside. Into the advancing darkness of the past. The war of youth was fought. But neither won nor lost. And now there is some time left to stare blankly and be strangely silent. I would say, "Alas" but there's no one to say it to and nothing to say it about. Alas.

Walking the Chasm #1. You can never return. No place is home twice. No eyes are the same. You can never escape your past. It follows relentlessly. I try to hide from mine all the time. I try to fake it out. Lose it on long flights to distant cities where I sit in small rooms and sweat. Days alone in stinking Bangkok. Walking night streets in African cities. I hide in books and dangerous distraction. It doesn't work. I find myself here. Hours after sunset. Hours before dawn. Alone in this night cubicle. My nocturnal introspective surveillance attempts to hide me from my lurking past. But it's no use. I always find myself with the waste, ruin, the dead. I wish it was different. I feel like I've somehow been able to limp away from some massive all consuming catastrophe that killed all the good ones. Left me here to measure my weakness against the strength of their absence. Dead people in my past. So many.

Seeing how isolated I am now, how did I ever know that many people? Was I different then? A loner waiting for these people to die off? I look at their letters, drawings, listen to their records. It's draining. There's nowhere to go but forward. Something about that feels like I'm running away. This room, all rooms—re-enforce the trembling smallness of life. All these sad, silent people. Undistracted. Somehow poisoned by intellect. Quietly knowing. Walking the chasm.

Walking the Chasm #2. Only by pushing mere existence until it screams and distorts does it become honest. Otherwise it gets soft. It hides and atrophies. Desperation keeps me honest. It's why I travel and work hard and put myself into situations I have to fight my way through. It's the only way I can reach truth. It is not an addiction. It is not because of compulsion or impulse but a dissatisfaction with the mediocre and easily understood. At this point, the information I seek can only be attained in extreme environments. Isolation. Exhaustion. Being away from that which is familiar. Being in situations in which I must utilize all I've got. I don't want a woman to be close to me. I don't want shelter from the storm. No kindness or perceived safety in intimacy do I seek. Many years ago I was different. Now I just want to walk the chasm.

No Shore #1. This is not a night. It is a sunken eternity. This is not a room. It is a horizonless morass. A doorless, four-walled ... thing. What is the time? I do not know. No clock. It is no o'clock. My heart is not a heart. It is an old machine that operates unnoticed with a weary, workman's efficiency. It is a steady but undetectable, purposeless clanging against the rusted hull of a ship surrounded by thousands of square miles of ocean. It was distractedly shoved aside. Marked redundant and immediately forgotten. There is a calm that arrives as soft and unnoticed as autumn after humiliation's ever hungry pack of hyenas have ripped the flesh away and crunched the bones to powder. There is a stillness and clear truth that is somehow truer than all other truths after regret and sorrow have incinerated desire and gently but firmly pinned obsession to the bottom of a pail filled with warm water until the kicking and thrashing ceased. There is a useless wisdom derived from the swift and damaging delivery. It is perhaps like an unnoticed moment of clarity in the last heartbeat of a life. A key that opens no door. Sky cracking thunder in a world gone deaf. And after all this existing in a conscious state of extinction, where to? Nowhere. Where are we headed? Nowhere. So go. Go to Nowhere. When you're here is nowhere, and your nowhere is all you can see—you've arrived. You're here. Nowhere. No need to look for welcome and no need to despair when it does not come. It will not come. Your only company is the sound of air and the microscopic monsters that run past the farthest corners of your periphery. There are no enemies here, no rivals, regulations, rates, time limit or minimum order. This is not life in life time, not breath-to-breath as causal link to eventual no breath-after-breath. Life has color, textural reference, mortality's unceasing forward march. This is not life. This is life on pause. Wheels turning in deep space. And still, that poor heart, like a dog struck by a car, dragging a broken leg, lungs filling with blood, limps back to the house so it can crawl under the porch and die unseen. That heart, seemingly immune to lessons taught, clangs steadily away against the rusted hull of the ship cast adrift... *someone to love ... someone to love me ... someone to love ... someone to love me ...* No direction, no stars, no daylight to come. There is no shore.

No Shore #2. All born dislocated amidst great distraction. But nothing keeps you from yourself for too long. In the heart of night when men quietly sweep the floors of empty dancehalls and the lonely walk back to silent rooms. There is no shore. When isolation turns you into the only one. And you become inescapable. And no words can be employed to explain or rationalize. And something inside you endlessly suffocates. Dies continuously. Starves and convulses. There is no shore. When someone's touch becomes narcotic. But provides no relief. Or gets you off. Or out of your mind. There is no shore. If I knew a name to call out, I would. Even though I know I am mute. And if there was a name to call. A cage of fleshed ribs to claw and hold onto. Mutually desperate arms to embrace me. A hot mouth on mine. It would not be relief or the end of panic. But only a temporary resting place. But the annihilating vacuum of constant life would be there to remind me. There is no shore. Two people in a darkened room. Two respirating carcasses imagining other carcasses. Each miles away in thought. No shore. People take years decorating the blank space. Addiction. Marriage. Children. They spend their lives working. Buying things to fill the space. But the more you put in the more you see. There is no shore. Drive faster. Make more noise. Tell yourself you're in love. Desperation's never ending mirage. Churches are built. Pyramids are left in deserts. Wars are fought. There is no shore. Future generations will struggle. With ever decreasing resources. They will read about the past with amazement and disbelief. They will wonder if their ancestors ever found it. After so much decimation. Conquering and culture erasing purges to clear all the sightlines and quiet the air. They will see. Those who came before them ripped the world to shreds and shook it apart yet huddled together in fear. Turned on each other in distrust. Ran wild intoxicated by ignorance. Found the voices of the evil and the righteous came from the same mouth. And no leader or prophet was able to lead them to the shore. In sleep I turn and grind my teeth. I know the truth but fight it. In waking hours I turn my head from the blank space and the past and wait for the night. For empty streets to walk lonely upon. Small rooms and solitude. For wind that rustles tree branches. For amnesia and darkness. There is no shore

No Shore #3. I went back to my hometown. I walked the old streets at night. There are no more lit rooms full of people. All the voices are long ago hushed and have been atomized by time. I walked lost down familiar streets. I was hoping to find something. I felt foolish, old and cowardly for wanting a connection to my past. I looked into the windows of my old house and saw a tall man in the living room. I walked down the alley and looked into my bedroom. It was dark. No one in that house knows me. I have no proof of myself. I paced those streets like a solitary cell. I looked in every corner for clues. If I stop trying to be found will I stop feeling so lost? Home is what I carry in my mind. It's not in someone's eyes or on an old street. It's nowhere to be found but inside. I am tired of running. I am embarrassed by my frustration at what I should have realized years ago. Beyond the confines of my thoughts and memories that run unheard and unknown to all but myself is where I live. There is no shore.

I stared into her eyes. Could this moment be like no other? Not ruined by ulterior motive? Not hammered by repetition? Not dulled by sheer exhaustion? Our steps, so weary. Our shoulders sore from the weight of disappointment. Could this time be different? Each breath a step into new life? Each word a drop in a newly discovered ocean? Am I brave enough to show myself? Does she wait in the clearing by the fire light? Does she wait for me? Does she know my name? Or is it just time falling straight down into humiliation, mortality and waste? Desire emboldened by disillusion? Fear of the darkness and time beyond the fire light? I've never seen the world in someone's eyes. Never saw my reflection in a smile. Is it you? Are you finally here? Fuck it. Solitary into this slow oncoming dark I go. Self-welcomed.

Maps, plans, itineraries and air tickets are better than your beauty and uncertainty. The slow change of seasons. Lizards running crookedly on brick and the night's insect choir are better than what you may or may not be. To be alone and know. To be cold and distant. To be unknown and in need is better than your mix of control and affection. There's no need for the long talks. There are no words that will keep me here. Nothing you offer or promise will turn my eyes back to you. North. South. East. West. Temperature and distance to destination doesn't make me suffer like you make me suffer. How could surrender to your embrace be anything other than exhaustion driven compromise?

I want to cut off ears and bleed paint. I want to be rich and multi-lingual. But not show it or let anyone know. I don't want to go to prison. But to already have done time in prison. For the street cred. I don't want to fight in a war. But to now be back from one. I want some cool scars. Given to me by a skilled surgeon. I want to kill people. Some in self defense. Some just to say I did. And not be lying. I want to lie most of the time. And never get caught. Because how it should be is way better than how it is. I want to see great works of literature with my name on the cover to spend unbelievably long periods of time on bestseller lists. Enraging my peers and detractors. When asked what I went through to write these works. I want to answer with a slight smile and shake of my head. The catch is, I don't want to do any of the writing. Writers are miserable bores. They get cancer. Their marriages fail. They are generally horrible and self-absorbed. They are better off living alone writing great books.

Letters to Whitey

07-22-02 Whitstable UK: 5:00 pm. Kill Whitey. Shalom, shadoobie, shattered. Hello! Whitey. Die. I'm in England. I go where the work is, where the white people are.

Today, I am transmitting from Whitstable, a small seaside town two hours out of London.

What's there to say about Whitstable? It is a small town on the fucked up Atlantic Ocean. It's a quaint haven for white vacationers (alcoholics) and the end of the line for fish as they are unceasingly wrenched from the filthy brine, beheaded, gutted, rolled in batter and hurled into cauldrons of boiling fat and inhaled still smoking down the cavernous gullets of both residents and visitors. It is a town full of white people. They could change the name to White Stable and it would fit like the barrel of a shotgun in the mouth of a crooked cop.

It's Monday. A day off. I got my mind on my kill whitey and my kill whitey on my mind. Tedium clogs the arteries. Orca Winfrey (Code white! Alert! Alert!) is on television with people who lost family members to the collapse of the World Trade Center. At this point, I don't see the good of wallowing in the misery and making these poor people cry for the millionth time just for ratings. How can Orca stand herself? Time to go.

I walked from this hotel room to the market to get some provisions for the night. I checked out my food options near the hotel and could not pass up the opportunity to jot down the contents of the chalkboard menu at the Seaside Café that exists not twenty paces from my dwelling. The Seaside

Café was closed when I was passed it earlier, perhaps they ran out of oil and couldn't fulfill the promise of said menu I will detail here:

Plaice, chips & peas

Cod, chips & peas

Scampi, chips & peas

2 sausage, chips & peas

2 sausage, egg & chips

Bacon, egg & chips

2 eggs & chips

Egg & chips

Egg, chips & beans

Ham, eggs & chips

Burger, egg & chips

Perhaps the cook ate the food and had a heart attack. Dealers shouldn't use their stash. But enough about the local cuisine, let's go shopping, shall we?

The walk to the market is a tricky one as for part of the journey, there's no sidewalk to ambulate upon, so one must take to the street and stay close to the wall to avoid traffic. This is not the difficult part. The frustrating constant is the pedestrians. Whether on the narrow strip of sidewalk or street side, they just stand, seemingly oblivious to the oncoming biped stomping towards them. When they finally take notice, it's only because they're getting knocked out of their placid, normal operating stupor by one hundred and eighty odd lean pounds of nonstopping market-bound mass. Perhaps this isn't the first time they've heard "Fuck outta my way," because they barely seem to notice my presence as they pick themselves up off the ground. No matter, gotta eat, gotta go to the market.

After several stores hawking antiques, chips, beans, pizza, alcohol, fish and fish catching equipment, there is a market in the form of a Somerfield. This is the second time I have been to this market and I'm much better prepared this time. The aisles of this market are clogged with fat children who seem to know the exact spots I want to be in because they trundle ahead of me and station themselves in those particular places and slouch with extreme uselessness and complete expendability. I never completely understood what Rodney Dangerfield meant when in Caddyshack, he looked at Spaulding and said, "Now I see why tigers eat their young." Now I do. On the previous visit to Somerfield, I was somewhat jet lagged and having seen George W Bush speak on television, felt the need to bolster up the sagging perception of Americans as rude, ignorant, double talking, white CEO's who can't speak in complete sentences by being polite to these obese mutant spawn. Wasting time, I said, "Excuse me," as I tried to reach around these greasy baby white whales for a red pepper. The usual response to this was a grunt and a vacant stare. So this time, I knew what to do. As I approached the mineral water section, I saw one of these creatures lurch towards the exact square of floor tile I planned to visit. By slightly changing my approach and walking in a semi-diagonal, almost sideways direction along the shelves, I was able to employ my hand basket as a kind of cow catcher and plow this piece of respirating excrement to the side and step into the spot it was occupying. Not even looking down to see what had happened, I selected and moved on. Looking for a roll of Trebor Extra Strong mints, I encountered two chubby darlings in their "I was molested by a white Catholic priest" school uniforms and managed to wipe them both out without even shifting the contents of my shopping basket. I plowed onto the check out line, paid the ancient woman, bagged my goods and left.

Back onto the sidewalk I went. One thing I can say for Whitstable, it sure makes me want to kick kids in the ass and kill whitey.

I get back to the hotel and look out at the ocean. Boy, the Atlantic sure has taken a beating over the centuries. This particular bit that now and again pays a withering salty visit to the shore has taken its leave again, receding back, how far back? Way back, back farther than Bono's hairline before the weave. Pasty fleshed children and gulls run around in that which the water has left behind—a green brown slime field. The shore is gray and brown rocks with a few park benches. At the benches, blazing white against the setting sun, are men in soccer jerseys and Adidas running shoes, drinking beer as they bravely try to enjoy their time by the sea. This is the view from my window. It is wretched.

A lot of people should keep their clothes on. There should be a sign instructing these "water users" (as they are referred to on the placards that line the gritty shoreline) that if they are over three hundred pounds (which seems to be a vast majority of the beach goers here), to please not wear swimming costumes that a child would normally wear. We really don't need to see all of that, do we? Green Peace should set up here and try to keep these people out of the water. You want to know where all the oil slicks are coming from? Well, now you do.

As the sun sets deeper and deeper into the miserable horizon, the Rosie O'Donnell sized sacks slowly get up, gather their belongings and stagger towards their vehicles. It's time to feed and as the water is long gone, there will be no plankton to be found so following their genetic imperative, they must go. As the mutants squeeze themselves into their cars, the night shift is arriving. Groups of moronic young white people, armed with no brains and beer will post themselves near my window so they can laugh and drink for the next six to seven hours.

Do you want to see the world's population eat daily? Do you want to see the end of conflict all over the world? Do you want to see the end of all this corny noise played by well-adjusted bitches that passes for music? Do you want a better life for you and yours? There's only one thing you have to do and all these petty ailments will cease abruptly. Kill Whitey.

08-04-02 London UK: 0026 hrs. Free your mind and your kill whitey will follow. Whitey. Blasting direct from London. When I got to London weeks ago I ventured into Tower Records and saw the cover of NME, that piece of shit pop music paper. The idiot from Oasis, (I know, which one) the singer idiot, was on the cover, holding a tambourine, looking lame (white). If you're a singer and you're holding a tambourine, you know you must die you white motherfucker. The cover of this corny publication said that you, yes you, could win Liam's tambourine! Can you imagine the white stampede after that prize? Kill whitey!

Days later, I was reading in some UK newspaper about a recent Oasis gig at a festival in Spain. The Spanish fans were apparently not into that special Oasis style of crap Beatles rip-off rock and let the band know it by hurling projectiles at Liam. Liam had to hide behind the backline! He got angry! He threw his tambourine into the seething mass underneath him! That will show them! Ha! The seething mass . . . they . . . they threw the tambourine back at him! Hey whitey, catch!

SO, if any of you chicken shit white motherfuckers want a tambourine that belonged to Liam, familiar to millions . . . (of cracker white bitches!) all you have to do is go to Spain where they are not all that interested in them. Fuck you whitey!!!!!!!

In other white news, the new Moby album cover sports Moby in an astronaut outfit as does his new video. The slant of the whole thing is that he's not from here. He's really far out. He's from another world. He's only visiting Earth because there's such a high population of white people. Oh yeah, I get it. He's really out there! He's about as "out there" as that bitch Jamiroquai (white). He's just another pop music maker. It's just pop music. No need to worry. Sun Ra is out there. George Clinton is out there. Jimi Hendrix is out there. Moby, you'll always be from the corporate "in there." Moby, you can take off the outfit now. Can you imagine Moby'ing your funk?! Ho! Can you imagine buying a Fat Boy Slim record? White people can.

I found myself on the streets tonight helping white people. Yes! They need help. They need training. The sidewalks were packed with white people. They changed lanes without using their indicators. They walked and then all of a sudden came to a lurching halt in the middle of the sidewalk to have a chat. This will not do. Whitey must be trained. Whitey must obey. Whitey is helpless and staggering from bar to bar. Whitey is obscene and lounging in decaying cities built by greed, lies, harnessed oppression and the hard labor of the working dead. Whitey must get smashed into by me. Whitey must get pushed along when whitey isn't moving fast enough on the sidewalk. Let's go! Whitey doesn't like getting prodded. Whitey better get used to it.

Whitey, each day you make the rope from which you will someday swing. You grow, buy and consume the tobacco that will someday blacken your lungs and give you cancer. You grow, manufacture, wait in line to buy and consume the fast-food that has turned your nation soft, sloth-like, diseased and easy to kill. You invent new medicines so you can live longer and poison yourselves for more years and someday sue the companies that provided the goods that you so eagerly consumed in mass quantities to toxify yourselves at the first possible opportunity. In the name of freedom, you have no one to blame but yourselves. War, ill health, debt, bad times...All you do is ask for it. And now, you got it! Die Imperialist Whitey Pig Dog Scum!!!!!!

Answer me these questions three:
    What do these three things have in common?
        (a) The White House
        (b) The White Cliffs of Dover
        (c) Creed
    Jim Carrey is as funny as ...
        (a) Child abduction
        (b) Cancer
        (c) Lethal injection
    What did we learn today?
        (a) Kill Whitey
        (b) Kill Whitey
        (c) Kill Whitey
Fuck you. (bonus track)

08-05-02 White Stable UK: Whitey hit me one more time! Whitey. I'm writing in hopes you're dead. If you are, cool. If you're not, read on. It's another Monday in White Stable. Hours ago, I set off into town once again to gather provisions for the long white night to come. It was another trip into the soft whitey underbelly.

The streets were more clogged than last time. Slow moving sea cows and their porcine spawn meandered along the narrow sidewalk, barely able to get their tremendous bulk around the white male lichen who can find no other place to stand and eat their gyros. I walked right through them. Problem? I'll kill you, you white motherfucker. Get in touch with your inner whitey and fear me. Fuck you.

Upon entering the market, I saw that it was more packed with dull, lifeless white people and their screaming, mongoloidal, coital spew than on my previous visit. The biological nightmare progeny of these useless shoppers immediately went for all the areas I needed to visit to block my access to the provisions I needed. This is a protective instinct. I can dig it. I have a few of my own. Kill whitey is probably the only one I need though.

Today, I employed a new strategy. Without looking at the demon gnomes running their water heads towards the food racks, I just locked eyes with the parents. I stared at them with a flat smile, my entire being screaming kill whitey. They got it. They scooped up these beasts and gave me room to work. Let your aura do the talking.

Check out is a whole new world of slow moving misery. No matter how much I tighten up the space between myself and the five foot wide shopper in front of me, an equally huge white one decides the break in the line to pass through is right in front of me. And this line will not move. The checkout woman is more lifeless than the Pope (white). Speaking of the Pope, why do white people still go in droves to see that guy? When you are the head whitey and it becomes known that the whiteys under your charge have been raping kids and their whitey peers have been covering their white asses, you have to answer some direct questions. He won't. There's never been a better time to kill whitey.

Anyway, the line was at a standstill and it reminded me of my most recent venture into my local Rite Aid for traveling supplies the last time I was in Los Angeles. (Los Angeles, city of whores, city of fat multi-millionaire record producers who meditate in their mansions, thinking it's going to get them in touch with something. City of porn-addicted white motherfuckers who wait, trembling in their beds knowing it's just a matter of time before Helter Skelter II comes down.) It was past midnight, a great time to go to Rite Aid because the place is full of freaks (whiteys we like). I am in line behind a couple. I am one transaction away from bringing my supplies to the counter. This will only take several minutes. The couple ahead of me is purchasing a heating pad. The price showing up on the man's receipt is not the lower marked price on the package. He is mad. His female freak counterpart tells him it's for his back and the money shouldn't matter. On this night, the freak was all about principle. The slack-jawed, sloth-like mutant woman behind the counter watches the two of them without even blinking. Another counter opens up. Bulimic women with fake tans, see-through tops and breast augmentation run over to the newly opened register, barely able to hold onto their cough syrup, condoms and beer. The man is steadfast and will not pay the extra one dollar and eighty-eight cents for the heat pad and must now fill out a long form that says he is voiding the charge on his credit card. I know, kill whitey! At that moment, a man walks into the Rite Aid, goes up to the cashier and with the classic up speak of those who should have been put in pails of warm water at birth says, "Excuse me? My brother is in the parking lot? And he fell on the ground? And he can't breathe? Can you please call an ambulance?" The cashier woman looks over at him and then back to the man filling out the form. I could go to another line but no, I am digging this way too much. The man with the asphyxiating brother starts in again. "Excuse me? My brother is in the parking lot? And he fell on the ground? And he can't breathe? Can you please call an ambulance? Thank you?" The cashier picks up her phone and with her lips moving about as much as a top billed ventriloquist, speaks. Her sleepy voice buzzes across the Rite Aid sound system. "9-1-1 call, register one." The man with the dead-by-now brother thanks her and leaves. Minutes later I am out of the Rite Aid and searching the parking lot for an ambulance or a dead guy on the ground. I find neither.

Minutes later I am out of the White Stable Somerfield and on the way to my next stop, the Woolworth's a few shops down to pick up some rolls of Trebor Extra Strong Spearmint Wafers. These are good. After about three, my mouth is in pain. It keeps my resolve up. Standing in front of the Trebor Extra Strong section are three children and a large female, all of them are white. All four of them moved when they saw me. Perhaps the several minute old legend of my rearrangement of the gyro eaters had spread.

Outside my window, white people are sitting on park benches on the stony beach eating fish and chips. Who ushered in the nuclear age? Who decided to keep sending troops to Vietnam? Who started Enron? World Com? Who's buying Linkin Park records? Who blows up kids in Northern Ireland? Why did whitey cross the road screaming, "Someone's trying to kill me?" When is <u>A Funny Thing Happened on the Way to the Uprising</u> coming out on DVD? Did you check out Michael Jackson's recent outburst? He's blaming Sony for the failure of his last record <u>Unlistenable</u>. Who did this child-tasting bleach boy bring with him to strike fear into the bloodless hearts of the Sony execs? Rev. Al Sharpton. They're still laughing. So am I. Kill whitey.

08-20-02 LA CA All White All the Time: It's whitey's world. I'm just running and ducking for cover all over it. Whitey, I am back in the filthy city of whores and how can I think of you and not be inspired to write? America's at war? Doesn't seem to be. Feels like the game is on. Whitey, answer me this and hope that I don't hitch you up to the back of my truck and drag you until your fucking head comes off. Who said the following statement recently:

"I am aware that, you know, some very intelligent people are expressing their opinions about Saddam Hussein and Iraq."

A. Woody Harrelson
B. Keanu Reeves
C. Bill O'Reilly (The O'Reilly Factor — A Show for White People)
D. Marianne Faithful (With Mick Jagger fifteen minutes, talked about it for fifty years.)
E. Sheryl Crow
F. Charlton Heston
G. Buffy the Vampire Slayer
H. The Duchess of York
I. Sean Combs
J. DJ Shadow
K. Ben Affleck

I bet you picked "H" and that was a pretty good choice but it was a trick question. The correct answer is George W Bush. The highest whitey of them all. He and his white staff get questioned about the impending or not impending invasion of Iraq all the time and they never have an answer that satisfies. Maybe Whitebush should listen to some of those "intelligent people" he, "you know," claims to be aware of. Perhaps he should have punctuated his sentence with the word "like" here and there to get that young white audience to pay attention, and finished it off with a questioning up-speak lilt to let people know that he knows and is like, going to take care it as in, "Like I am aware that, you know, like some very intelligent people are expressing their opinions about Saddam Hussein and Iraq?" See, just a few changes and President Whitey comes across like one of his alcoholic daughters. We have communication, we have crossover, we have customers. This is the same way tobacco companies work. Basically, America, let's party. But you know what

Rush Limbaugh says, "Democrats, the party's over." Ya got that right, doper!

12-17-03: It's almost Christmas Whitey! Did ya read the article by Merle Hekmatyar in American Jihadist? Awesome! You know, one of these days, someone's just going to come up and shoot you in the face. It's what they do with terrorists! Viva la causa fuckhead! Sen. Trent Lott says he "said the wrong thing to the wrong people" in praising Strom Thurmond's 1948 segregationist presidential candidacy which also supported lynching of blacks by white citizens for fun, but the controversy continues amid indications from White House advisers that President Bush won't try to save Lott's job because he's running for re-election in 2004 and can't have Lott screw it all up just because he talked out of class.

The White House position could seal Lott's fate because a number of GOP senators are expressing concerns that the Klan supporting Mississippi senator is a liability to their hidden agenda to keep the black race at bay. Tuesday afternoon, Bush maintained the silence he has kept on the matter since Thursday, waving off a reporter's question about whether Lott could still lead effectively. Mr. Bush often waves off reporters because it's easier than answering the question and he's not good at speaking spontaneously or speaking at all really. He's got enough on his mind with his daughters out running amok and getting all the men they can eat. And then there's the problem with Iraq and "that other one that's not Iraq. So many weird names. Why can't these faggoty rag headed bastards have names like Doug and Bart and cities that are easy to say like Texas?" Bush commented days before.

Meanwhile, Bush met at the Whitey House Tuesday with House Speaker Dennis Hastert, proceeding without Lott to plan for the 2003 congressional hidden agenda to keep the black man's forward progress hopelessly at a standstill. Whitey House spokesman Ari Fleischer said Lott, at home in Mississippi, was not excluded for any political reason. "For us to talk with anybody from the Senate, they need to be in Washington—that's the fucked up, pussy-ass excuse we have for not answering that question at this time." Fleischer remarked with uncharacteristic candor, usually reserved for a drunken Donald Rumsfeld.

As for the date set to decide Lott's fate, Fleischer made clear that Bush will not intervene either for or against Lott. "The Whitey House won't comment on that meeting or anything that could reveal the Whitey House's leading up to anything that would in any way have the most remote semblance to a straight answer on that or any other topic at this time or any time in the foreseeable future," Fleischer said.

Trying to salvage what's left of his political career, Lott reached out Monday to the community he now admits he prefers segregated, and tried to give the illusion to black Americans that minorities could benefit from his continued leadership.

"I accept the fact that I made a terrible mistake, timing is everything and that was the wrong time to say those words. Those statements weren't to be heard by coloreds at any time," Lott, R-Miss., said during a 30-minute interview with Black Entertainment Television. "But it is about actions more than words. Nobody got lynched and no crosses were burned as far as I know. As majority leader I can move an agenda outwardly displaying aspects that would hopefully be thought of as helpful in the minds of African Americans and minorities of all kinds and to real Americans too."

Lott has been trying to spin his Dec. 5 toast to centenarian Sen. Strom Thurmond, when he publicly wished that Thurmond had been elected president in 1948. Mississippi voted for Thurmond, Lott recalled, "and if the rest of the country had followed our lead, we wouldn't have had all these problems over all these years either. White Power!"

Thurmond's third-party platform in 1948 was almost wholly segregationist, upholding bans on multiracial marriages and the defense of the South from "anti-lynching" reforms.

Bush's political advisers say they are highly disappointed with Lott's explanations, but say they had been ordered by the President not to take any overt or covert action against the Mississippi Republican. Bush has shown in the past it's often easier to do nothing about a situation.

The Whitey House faces a dilemma: Lott is hurting both Bush and his party, but any effort to take down Lott will hurt Bush with his white Southern base, say senior Republicans close to the Whitey House. Bush also feels some loyalty toward Lott, but will burn him in a second if he thinks the darkie vote will be of more help to him in 2004 Whitey House officials said.

Thus, the president's political team is forced into what one Whitey House official between hiccupping bursts of laughter, called "the good old strategy of silence," hoping events themselves lead to Lott's removal or - much less likely - somehow end the controversy.

Sen. Don Nickels, R-Okla., Lott's longtime rival within the GOP leadership, was the first Republican to break ranks over the weekend and call for new leadership elections, and there were fresh signs of Lott's political weakness Monday. The Republican National Committee maintained its silence about the controversy, and the Whitey House issued its sharpest rebuke yet.

Fleischer said Lott's remarks about Thurmond's presidential bid were "offensive and repugnant to certain groups of people, pathetic and sad to other groups, wildly funny to others and yet to other other groups, right down the line straight ahead common sense. I think that covers the Whitey House's ass pretty well." At the same time, Fleischer repeated on Tuesday, "Again, the president thinks there's no need for him (Lott) to resign. There's a lot of good old boys in the Senate and most of them are, well, good old boys."

Some colleagues rallied behind Lott. Incoming GOP whip Sen. Mitch McConnell, R-KY., repeated his support for Lott on Monday, saying he hoped "this issue is resolved quickly so we can move forward together to advance the president's agenda of selling out the black man conveniently, efficiently and as often as possible."

Sen. Judd Gregg, R-N.H., called the remarks "exceptionally inappropriate, he didn't go into detail about what problems these coons have caused over the years." but said they should be placed in context with what he called Lott's "provincial way of thinking".

Democrats are discussing a rare censure motion against Lott, and several have said he should consider stepping down.

Lott's reputation suffered as much from his toast - which he said was ill-timed - as it did from the subsequent analysis of his political record, and his state record for number of crosses burned in one county in one year which showed resolved opposition to causes dear to the civil rights community and anyone with a sense of human decency.

In his fourth apology-spin to date, Lott scrambled to show he was a changed man. He announced that he now supports making Martin Luther King Jr.'s birthday a federal holiday - having voted against it on the Senate floor - and said he supports affirmative action and anything else that will get the blacks to shut up already.

"I'm for affirmative action and I've practiced it," he said. "I've had African Americans on my staff, in my stables, out in my fields and around the house along with other minorities, but particularly African Americans, since the mid-1970s. Coloreds have stronger backs and can work longer hours. Orientals are smarter but complain more."

Some Republican aides speculated about an effort to coax Lott from his leadership with the prospect of a committee chairmanship, or a sweet position in the Tobacco Industry. They worry that a humiliated Lott could resign his Senate seat, start naming names, gettin' the boys together, burning crosses and hitching up the rope to his father's oak tree, allowing Mississippi's Democratic governor to name a Democratic replacement - and leaving the Senate at a 50-50 tie.

04-06-05 **Whitey Power Supremacist Matthew "In Jail" Hale gets 40 years!!!! Oh Whitey there's a riot goin' on!! My friends Jacob, Luther and Ahmed are on their way over and we're going to listen to the Straight Outta Compton album all night long!** Matt, do the men who line up to pack your ass call you Pontifex Maximus like the "followers" of your "church" did? World Church of the Creator? Whitey's better than everyone else?! Whitey's on the run?! Whitey's being hunted down and killed by those Jew bastards?! Matt?

Matt, let me get this straight. White people are the creators of all worthwhile culture and civilization? Nonwhites are the natural enemies of the Whitey race? Wow!

Matt, it's ok to be an idiot and preach your bullshit to the dumb motherfuckers who have nothing else to do but rape their kids, pollute their bodies and listen to you spew. People sit and listen to idiots give speeches all the time. Hell, even I watched the last State of the Union Address. It's not ok to try and get a judge you disagree with killed. Matt, this is America! Land of the free! It's not how we're doing business! It's why you walked your dumb ass into court and got arrested and sent away. It's why they found you guilty! It's why you're going to get out when you're in your 70's! How will your asshole survive the blitzkrieg of cock that is no doubt on its way?! "Mein holen ist swollen!!"

I read about your old website that had educational games for kids. Kids love games! One of the games you had, a fill-in-the-blanks kinda thing, right? I found two examples:

"The _____ are the deadliest enemies of the White Race"

"_____ was the greatest White Leader that ever lived."

Oh Matt, you cut-up! I made up one of my own! Here goes: Whitey Supremacist psycho, _____, overstepped his bounds and is going to spend 40 years in jail!!!!

Can ya guess the answer?!

I love this quote of yours: "The WCOTC is the most dynamic and inspiring organization in existence for the survival, expansion, and advancement of our beloved White Race." What are ya, a goose-stepping L Ron Hubbard without the ascot?! You cultists are a scream! What's Tom DeLay's home number?

Here's another red hot zinger of yours—love it!!: "The mud races may very well offer some resistance and that resistance will have to be destroyed." I think those "mud races" are going to be buying you for three cigarettes!

Matt, I just found this incredible "interview" of yours on the White Struggle website. It's more like an infomercial for complete lunacy. By the way, how many showers did it take to get Ann Coulter's spit off your dick? Anyway, this is my favorite bit of your "chat" with Kathy Robertazzo. It's like an infomercial from Hell. Hell, Matt, HELL! I guess this was conducted before you got sent to prison for 40 years. Is it 40 years? Hold on, let me check. Yep! 40 years!

KR: How is your political campaign going, and if you win your bid for city commissioner, what kind of changes do you have in your sights?

MH: Well, the first thing is to keep East Peoria an all White town. Currently we are 98% White. I want to produce more jobs for White people. I want to make sure our children are getting the proper education.

KR: Are you going to insist the school system stop teaching lies about the holocaust and portraying Martin Luther King as a hero instead of the adulterer and communist he was?

MH: Yes, that would be a start.

KR: A lot of people don't realize the Jews were behind the civil rights movement as just another effort to bring down the White man, how do you see it?

MH: Absolutely, the Jews founded the NAACP and in fact a Jew ran that organization until 1975. By empowering the black man they would destroy the White man.

Matt! Stunning. Completely amazing. It's funny to read this stuff now, knowing you're in a cage with your ass leaking but man, the level of your insanity is hard to get one's head around. The part where you think you're going to be President is hysterical. America's made some bad choices in that department, you never know. Can you imagine how we feel knowing that our tax dollars are paying for your food and anal sutures when we could be buying flak vests for our brave men and women in the Armed Forces?

Matt, can we take a minute here to discuss this White Struggle website? On the left side, there's a series of topics listed. The one that jumped out at me first was titled "Blacks Actually Owe the US." I clicked on it and was taken to What About African America's Debt? Time To Tell The Vocal Charlatans To Shut Up by William Mayer. It reads like The Onion on PCP! By way of some Enronesque accounting, Mayer figures African Americans are in debt to America and should shut up because in America their chances of getting eaten alive by a lion or a crocodile is next to nil. Mr. Mayer sums it all up in the last line of his piece "The time has long past for the majority in this society to tell these relatively few but vocal charlatans to shut the hell up and start working for it like everyone else - the price has been paid in extremis - you owe us." Mr. Mayer is also the editor and publisher of Pipe Bomb News. Matt, do you think they'll let you out for your parents' funerals? You're going to be in so long they'll both die while you're inside.

Another title bar, "The Auschwitz Fraud", took me to The Auschwitz Fraud: From 9,000,000 Dead Jews To 38,031. No one took authorship of this one. Some more creative accounting takes the number of Jews killed at Auschwitz down to a mere 38,031. Whew! All this time I had thought Nazis were so bad and now to know they only killed little over thirty-eight thousand Jews at Auschwitz! Why, the Nazis weren't so bad after all! Hugs all around!

Matt, Matt, Matt. The world you live in is so completely horrible and white. It's so terrifying and negative and wrong and evil. 40 years. It should be 4000.

Matt, I know you know this but let me remind you: You're never going to win. Cowards never win. They'll always attract some weaklings but at the end of the day, you're all viewed as what you are. Dangerous lunatics.

As you pace your cell, do you ever stop and say out loud, "I am such a fuck up! I have thrown my life away!"? You have Matt. You have thrown your life away and I couldn't be happier.

You might have made a good soldier for Osama bin Laden. You two seem to have a few things in common. Actually, you lack the toughness to withstand the Al Queda training and they don't have time for pussies like you. Hang yourself tonight. Stop wasting food.

05-05-05 Whitey Alert! Laura Bush drops trou and pisses in the punch at the White House Correspondents' Dinner! Get down girl! Your husband's going to jail! But before he goes, a few laughs!: Laura Bush's White House Correspondents Dinner Notes/Rough Draft. I am married to the President of the United States and here is our typical evening: Nine o'clock, Mr. Excitement here is sound asleep, and I am watching Desperate Housewives with my thighs wrapped around Lynne Cheney's head as she delicately nibbles my clitoris. Ladies and gentleman, I am a desperate housewife and the first Lady, so Lynne HAS to do me first! But she's into it. I mean if those women on that show think they're desperate, they ought to be with George, what a fucking dud. Thank god Condi turned me onto same sex relationships! Dr. Rice, as she likes to be called when she's in Dominatrix mode, is a very generous lesbian as well as being a damned good liar.

One night after George went to bed, Lynne Cheney, Condi Rice, Karen Hughes and I got a room at the Hilton. I wouldn't even mention it except Ruth Ginsberg and Sandra Day O'Connor saw us there and joined in. I won't tell you what happened, but Lynne's Secret Service codename is now "Born Again Lesbian." I guess she and her daughter have a lot to talk about now. I think that's sweet.

George always says that he's delighted to come to these press dinners. Bullshit. He's hates you people because he's not as smart as any of you and he knows it and he's tired of embarrassing himself every time he gets words wrong. He has no problem lying to your face though, he doesn't think you all deserve the truth. He doesn't look at the stats regarding the number of American boys and girls coming home dead or torn apart. He can't handle it. He knows what he's doing. He knows he's made a big mistake and he knows he's a war criminal and a liar. He knows he's hated and he knows there's a lot of voter regret and that he'd lose to Kerry if everyone was allowed to vote again. He also knows that all you correspondents are a bunch of fucking cowards and won't confront him.

George and I are complete opposites. I'm a literate woman who values truth, my vibrator and valium. My husband is a horrible man with no guts and no integrity at all. I'm introverted, clinically depressed and on medication, he's extroverted and manic. I can pronounce 'nuclear.' I can read. The list goes on folks.

The amazing thing is that George and I were just meant to be. I was a les ... librarian **(pause for laughter if there is any, gauge crowd)** who spent 12 hours a day in the library, yet somehow I met George. There was a bar around the corner I used to see him standing in front of. He exposed himself to me as I drove by and I thought he was cute and pulled over. We've been together ever since. He's dumb as a post but he's my post! But seriously folks, George and I are unique in the Bush Family in that our marriage wasn't arranged by his mother.

People often wonder what my mother-in-law is really like. People think she's a sweet, grandmotherly Aunt Bea type. She's actually more like J. Edgar Hoover with a dick. You wonder how George's dad ever got the inspiration to shack up with her. Can you imagine sex with that furry beast? I'd rather try and get through the Patriot Act!

I'm proud of George. He's learned a lot about ranching since that first year when he tried to milk the horse. What's worse, it was a male horse. But seriously folks, he's been jacking off Halliburton execs since he was governor. He perfected his stroke on assorted Saudis. He used to "milk" Prince Abdullah but now they're just casual friends and hold hands. But what do I know? I'm just his fuckin' wife!

Now, of course, he spends his days clearing brush, cutting trails or taking down trees. The girls call it, "Operation No Tree Left Behind." Aren't those two a fuckin' failure?! They're drunk a lot of the time. They chuck empties into his wood chipper and yell, "One for Saddam!" whenever some flying debris hits him in the head. They're going to end up like their dad, a soft handed rich kid with a wicked sense of entititlement **(pause for laughter)**. George's answer to any problem at the ranch is to cut it down with a chainsaw, or have one of his illegals do it. Which I think is why he, Cheney and Rumsfeld get along so well. They all like to destroy things that don't belong to them and call it progress and they love cheap labor. Aren't I a funny bitch?! Lynn, a little to the left! By the end of 2007, there won't be a damn tree left in the country and there'll be a bunch of those faggoty liberals saying, 'I told you so!'

It's always very interesting to see how the ranch air invigorates people when they come down from Washington to visit. Vice President Cheney visited us lately. He got up early one morning, emerged from his bunker, put on his hiking boots, and went on a brisk, 20 to 30 foot walk and then was evacuated to a secret location. He has a persecution complex, he thinks everyone hates him!

But seriously folks, I do love the ranch, and I love the whole Bush family. I was an only child, and when I married into the extended Bush-Saudi Klan, I got brothers and sisters and wonderful in-laws, all of whom opened their arms to me. And included in the package, I got this guy here. Oh well! At least I didn't have marry jiggly Jeb! **(pause for camera whip to Jeb Bush).**

I think when you marry someone, you are subconsciously looking for something in your spouse to help fill, I mean <u>fulfill</u> **(proceed through laughter and applause)** something in you, and if George had a few more inches, he could do that for me. Boo-ya! He at least brought fun and energy into my life and so many other things, like a lot of money he didn't earn but got to keep anyway! Hello folks, I'll be here for the next four years, please award my husband's friends no bid contracts generously! **(pause for reaction, get ready to evacuate).**

06-22-05 Edgah! Edgah Rayyyyyyyyyy!!!!! Time to go to jail you fuckin' cracker!! Took a few decades but you're finally going away, you Whitey Supremacist piece of shit. The jury was nine whites and three blacks and you still got nailed! Must have been surprising. Justice for Chaney, Goodman and Schwerner.

I just found this online Whitey, read on!

Robb: Covered Gasoline Soaked Rags and On Fire in NYC
By Ahmed Jackson

NEW YORK CITY (AP) — Hours after Edgar Ray Killen's conviction, Klan leader and stand up comedian, Thomas Robb finds humor in Manhattan club.

Pastor Thomas Robb, national director of the Ku Klux Klan also perhaps America's most popular White Supremacist comic, part of the White Robe Comedy Tour and writer and star of his one white man show "Trapped in the Body of a White Man," zinged a Manhattan New York nightclub audience hours after Edgar Ray Killen's sentencing hearing. The audience was howling. The performance shows that not even the sentencing of one of his closest friends could keep Robb from tearing it up in the big apple.

"If anything, they convicted Edgar out of fear of retaliation. You can see a juror down in Mississippi whose name and address was to be published, fearful of not appeasing the black minority, not that anyone in Mississippi can read! But seriously folks, I'm a self-made man. I skin my own possum and only fuck my own kids! Hey now!"

"Really folks, a lot of people see the Klan as 'ignorant baboons or super geniuses intent on controlling the world'! I see some of you baboons in the back are offended! Now we might have been the first ones to successfully rape a four year-old girl but we're not exactly cut out for controlling the world. That's for you New York Jew boy lawyers! Git'r done!"

For a solid forty-five minutes, Robb had the audience gasping for breath.

"I tell you, if Bush were in the Klan, we wouldn't have all the problems we do now! White Power!"

Robb had to stop for a several seconds as laughter and applause thundered through the club while an endless barrage of drinks, coins and tins of Skoal hit the stage.

"I'm not saying nobody in the Klan has ever committed a crime. That's like saying no one in New York has ever committed a crime. People have no idea that members of the Klan generally have a higher than average income and educational level. Now I'm gonna go backstage and do some Oxy with Rush. White power! Good night!"

And then he was gone as more drinks and a stuffed possum (!) hit the stage. Only in New York, folks!

Whitey, you have to wonder how you're still alive after all you've done. If anyone hanged your father and didn't do any time, you would have gone berserk. Imagine how you're going to feel with a rag in your mouth as a man in a ski-mask saws your fuckin' head off?

05-15-04 Allahu Akbar Whitey! Westside Mullahs rock the mic on time! Get the fuck up and feel the bass!! Century City Mujahideen is up in this bitch! I had heard about a booklet offered by the office of Utah Senator Orrin Whitey Hatch on how to help parents deal with their children's drug use and/or the prevention thereof. Some of the things I had heard said about the book seemed too hilarious even for the Hatchter (he's the one who wants the ass grabbing freak Arnold Whitenegger to be President). One journalist told me he called the white Senator's office to try to obtain a copy and was brushed off. Recently my prayers were answered when I obtained a copy of the amazing How Parents Can Help Children Live Marijuana Free published in 1997. It features an introduction by the Hatch man himself!

The Senator's introduction has dazzling insight and will no doubt be useful to parents not only in Utah, but in America as well. Following are some highlights where the Senator breaks it down. First, he warns of the plague that is covering America in a suffocating blanket of moral decay and utter reefer madness. Word to your Imamma!!

"Dear Parents,

A plague, unprecedented in its impunity, is sweeping across the school-yards, playgrounds and streets of America. Its victims are our children. With the support of a morally deprived society that has chosen to embrace, rather than attack, this plague, the abuse of marijuana has embedded itself in the culture of America's youth. Marijuana use among young people is up a staggering 141 percent since 1992. Even more troubling, these users are getting younger and younger."

It's a damned plague. All the deaths from marijuana use. Why can't America's youth just stick to Oxycontin, booze and tobacco and let the good folks of Utah get back to their forgery, blood atonement and polygamy?!

"A culture of disdain that had firmly taken root in the 1990s, has been replaced by the glorification of this harmful drug by the entertainment industry, media and pro-legalization zealots, with no regard for the harm inflicted upon society by their actions. The casualties of these actions are the youth of America."

The youth of America?! They're the ones coming back with their limbs blown off or worse, from the wars Whitey starts but can't finish. Infidels step off!

Orrin says that parents must take action or there may be no tomorrow for the children of this generation! Is he talking about pot or if they bring back the draft?

"The future of this nation is dependent upon a total commitment from society to reject the drug scourge plaguing our nation's youth. As parents, it is our moral responsibility to take aggressive, uncompromising actions to help navigate our children through the destructive web of marijuana abuse. This book will serve as your map on this journey."

It's one destructive web, alright. Right up there with politicians who lie, outsourcing of employment, prescription drug abuse (Hey now, that's only for the parents and right wing talk show hosts!) As if marijuana was the only problem facing our nation's youth! How about teaching them how to read? Have you heard Bush speak? Talk about the child who got left behind! Makes you want to roll a fat one and build a mosque. Hit me!

I always thought marijuana use was a waste of time because when you're high, you can't see the evil workings of Whitey. I think you should never get stoned so you can be sharp and strong. You don't want to be high when it's time to watch Bush and Cheney get thrown in jail with Saddam, Milosevic and Ken Lay. You gotta be awake to jump up and down and kick holes in Sean Hannity's door. I don't want anything to take the edge off. I hate Whitey too much to get high. I don't drink his alcohol, I don't smoke his tobacco, I don't eat his body-killing food, I don't buy into his fear trips, I see though his cowardice and lies every day. I don't want to be off balance. I want to remove these cowards from power and you can't do it high. As far as that moral decay that Hatch goes on about, it seems you might need to smoke out when enduring the pressures of a three wife marriage! I think the marijuana plague will peter out on its own anyway. In a few years, when we're a Muslim nation, the penalties for marijuana use and possession will be so harsh, it won't be worth it. We'll be too busy stoning our wives and chopping the hands off thieves to get high! Who's your Mullah?!

This booklet is an eye opener for sure! I wanna be a doctor too!

"Doctors know that two "joints" do as much damage to the lungs as an entire pack of cigarettes."

"Regular marijuana users center their lives on its use. They become dependent upon the drug. When they are not high, they are either thinking about it or recovering from its effects."

"Most marijuana users who do advance to harder drugs are already addicted to marijuana and are looking for a stronger high."

Plot loss, confidence and balls like Rumsfeld pre-invasion! Come on with your Jihad, woman!

"Most marijuana consumed in the United States is imported from foreign countries by hardened criminals whose only concern is maximum profit."

Smoke American dope you fuckin' hippies! Support California. Governor Assengrabber needs all the help he can get. Eat American fast-food when abroad! Talk about hardened criminals whose only concern is maximum profit. Orrin, you white, white man, you. Time for you to shake the tree they live in and watch so many of your friends and campaign contributors fall out!

"Marijuana also has been considered as a potential appetite stimulant for people with AIDS. Marijuana was believed to counteract the loss of appetite and result-ant extreme weight loss suffered by AIDS patients. AIDS activists and some physicians also believed that mari-juana counteracts the effects of nausea suffered by AIDS patients. However, there is no firm evidence that mari-juana stops this wasting syndrome; in fact, this poten-tial use of marijuana has not been clinically tested."

Well then test it, ya lazy bastard! What are ya waiting for, all the AIDS suf-ferers to die off?! The Bush Administration, the most homophobic one since Regan's, should test marijuana on AIDS patients like insurgents are testing

IED's on American soldiers. Treat them like convicts or lab animals. A lot of Christians will love it! All the AIDS sufferers can be sent off to an island to infect and care for one another with all the confiscated marijuana. All those horrible queers (Cheney's daughter included) and other deviants can all die together and everything will get better and better and we can get back to our AA meetings, lap dances and gun homicides.

Nothing in the book prepares the reader for the amazing chapter **WARNING SIGNS OF MARIJUANA USE**. Are you ready? Here we go!

MEDICAL SYMPTOMS OF REGULAR USERS

-Appears lazy
(President Bush)

-Chronic, hacking cough—like a heavy tobacco smoker's.
(Tobacco smokers, people with tuberculosis.)

-Chronic fatigue
(Me by the last page of <u>How Parents Can Help Children Live Marijuana Free</u>.)

-Weight Loss
(Millions of starving people all over the world.)

-Chronic sore throat
(Lemmy)

-Disturbed menstrual cycles
(Ann Coulter, Karl Rove)

-Dry Mouth
(Very thirsty people.)

-Eyes sensitive to light—users may have a "squinty" appearance.
(Albinos, detainees.)

-Red Eyes
(Vampires, Dick Cheney Sunday morning)

-Frequent headaches
(The President's speech writers.)

-Impaired coordination caused by a distorted sense of time.
(You got me there. What the fuck are you talking about?)

-Moves and speaks in slow motion (like a "zombie").
(John Kerry)

BEHAVIORAL SIGNS OF REGULAR USERS

-Abrupt mood changes for no apparent reason.
(All women are regular marijuana users.)

-Antagonistic to all authority
(Iraqi insurgents are regular marijuana users.)

-Belligerent
(I'm a regular marijuana user? Mighty Allah, say it ain't so!)

-Depressed
(The US Economy is a regular marijuana user.)

-Evasive
(Condoleezza Rice is a regular marijuana user.)

-Excessively private
(Dick Cheney is a regular marijuana user.)

-Lack of motivation to much of anything, especially anything physical. (This is not normal in teenagers.)
(All teenagers are regular marijuana users.)

-Lying
(George W Bush is a regular marijuana user.)

-Marked decrease in personal hygiene. (This is also not normal in teenagers).
(All people in Baghdad now without water and electricity are regular marijuana users.)

-Memory loss
(Ronald Regan was a regular marijuana user.)

-Problems at school, talk of dropping out.
(All highschool students and children left behind are regular marijuana users.)

-Sneaky
(Tom DeLay is a regular marijuana user.)

-Sudden, precipitous drop in grades.
(Children with ADD are regular marijuana users.)

-Sudden loss of previous interests, especially sports.
(All goth kids are regular marijuana users.)

-Very sloppy or extreme dress and grooming. (Boys tend
to have long and/or unkempt hair. Girls may wear
extreme and/or revealing clothing. Both may sport sunglasses to hide red eyes.)
(Wow, let's see. The cast of "Cats", Kiss, Brittany Spears, Cher, Phil Spector,
Donald Trump, Sports Illustrated swimsuit issue models, strippers, porn
stars, Olympic swimmers and many people wearing sunglasses are regular
marijuana users.)

SOCIAL SIGNS OF REGULAR USERS
(This is the best one of them all!)

-Avoids the family while at home.
(All kids home for the holidays are regular marijuana users.)

-Interest in Ras Tafari (sic) religion. (Marijuana use
is part of that religion.)
(A healthy interest Satanism is ok though. Most Satanists are White
Infidels and will be burning in hell anyway so who cares about burning a
few doobies on the way? La Allah illa Allah!)

-Extreme rebelliousness a la James Dean in "Rebel
Without a Cause".
(When your kid is beating your brains out of your nose with one of your
golf clubs, it's a good chance he's on meth. All people who have seen "Rebel
without a Cause" are regular marijuana users. You can pick them out
easy—they're the trouble makers asleep in front of the TV, covered in
Doritos™.)

-Excessive preoccupation with social causes, race rela-
tions, environmental issues, etc.

(All liberals, philanthropists and civically responsible people suffering from
extreme cases of common sense and human decency are obviously regular
marijuana users.)

-Frequent, lengthy, or unexplained absences.

(All survivors of alien abductions are regular marijuana users.)

-Runs away or threatens to.

(All children trying to escape molestation by a parent or relative are regular marijuana users.)

-Serious sibling conflicts.

(Everyone with a sibling is a regular marijuana user.)

-Stays out all night or comes in at abnormally late
hours.

(People too drunk to find their way home are regular marijuana users.)

-Camp-outs and stay-overs (to distance themselves from
parents.)

(All boy scouts and boys who to go Neverland Ranch are regular marijuana
users.)

-Unacceptable new friends or refusal to bring new
friends home.

(All uncool parents and self-conscious teens are regular marijuana users.)

-Vocabulary is full of drug culture slang. (see the
Appendix, page 56)

Oh let's!

DRUG SLANG - Vocabulary for Parents - "4:20, I Be Feenin'"

Many drug-related slang expressions like "dealer," "high," and "narc" have entered everyday teenage slang. Parents need not worry if they hear them. But some slang terms refer expressly to marijuana and its use. You will find many of them defined here. Occasionally use of such slang does not automatically brand a teenager as a drug user, but frequent use of words in this list should be a "red flag" to parents.

Some of my favorites that I have heard my "homies" use:

BAG: A variable amount of marijuana sold in a plastic sandwich baggie. The actual amount is usually specified. A dime bag sells for 10$. Half-a-dime bad is a nickel bag. Sometimes bags are sold as two- or three-finger bags, describing how full the baggie is.

DEAL: Sell marijuana to another user.

DRUGGIE: Someone who looks and acts like a regular drug user or is high all the time. Also called a burnout, head, freak, stoner or stoney.

FEENIN': Desperate to get high (Black slang).

4:19 OR 4:20: "Let's go get high."

FREAK OUT: Behavior of someone so high they cannot control them selves. Antonym: chill or maintain.

HIT: A single inhalation of marijuana. Verb: to smoke (a joint or pipe). "Let's hit a bowl of my homegrown."

CIRCUMSTANTIAL EVIDENCE OF MARIJUANA USE:

-Sickly sweet odor of burning hemp on hair, clothing, and breath; drug culture clothing; posters; and music. (Some music and rap groups specialize in lyrics that are explicitly drug oriented.) Listen to the words. CDs and tapes containing lots of drug songs should be dead give-aways. Clothing and posters may contain pro-drug slogans and pictures or pictures of marijuana leaves or plants. Marijuana users also like to look at "black-light posters" while high.

(Not for the last 30 years, but no doubt these parents will remember getting stoned out of their minds and looking at them for hours.)

-Hours on the internet. You may believe that your children are safe from marijuana when they are working on a computer. Don't be too sure! If you have a computer hooked up to the internet, your children can interact with individuals who promote pro-marijuana beliefs, get information on how to grow marijuana and even purchase all types of marijuana paraphernalia—including seeds. "Chat rooms" are especially dangerous because unsuspecting children can be lured into believing the content of pro-marijuana messages. Remind your children that very disreputable people can say anything they want to because no one is checking for accuracy. Parents must prevent

their children from gaining access to these pro-marijuana Internet sites.

(Damn right you should be careful of disreputable people who say anything they want because no one is checking for accuracy. What is THE FOX NEWS CHANNEL? —That's correct! You win the lounge set and we won't draft your son!)

Whitey, maybe it's time for you to take the bullshit by the horns and do the hard work. The hard work entails building a country that values border security as a deterrent as valuable as all this morality crap and the letter of the law. It also involves admitting that America is an addicted consumerist culture and if it has a price tag on it, someone will inevitably find value in it and want to possess it. Cars, drugs, anything. Politicians, lawmakers and all the hypocrites who huddle in churches with their morals on display and their scandals in the papers will have to admit that they are part of the reason why their children take drugs.

Whitey, how did I avoid the self-destructive crisis of drug abuse? I was surrounded by it, waist deep in it. It was not a matter of how, it is a matter of why. Because I am full of fuckin' hate and I don't want to be like you. I don't want to end up dependent on common toxins like marijuana and easy credit. Drugs are just another way you enslave.

It's not surprising that you focus on marijuana to make an embarrassing booklet (that you won't even give to the press) and not attack truly dangerous drugs like crystal methamphetamine, heroin, and cocaine. If nothing else, the booklet shows your almost total disconnect with young people and people below a middle class income.

You drive local law enforcement crazy as they chase down small dealers and get shot at for their trouble but you won't address the reasons why people sell drugs: It's because they're like you—looking for a good profit.

Drugs provide escape. You preach escape in every possible media at every possible opportunity. Escape, denial and hypocrisy are your stock and trade yet you punish those who partake. You have sex in almost every advertisement and then you have police women pose as prostitutes to lure men to them so you can arrest them. Crime and Punishment is good business so you keep it going. If the crime rate drops below a certain level, no doubt, you'll find a way to fix that.

You decry addiction but the economy relies on addiction to sustain itself. America is a doped nation. Millions of Americans self-medicate on prescription drugs, alcohol, tobacco and fast food (but that's alright because you own the companies). Just one addiction to another but as long as they keep buying then all is well.

White collar addictions are ok. They are clean and your profit margin is assured. Street drugs sold by nonwhites are a problem because you don't profit. Non-whites get jail time and Whitey gets interventions, hugs, rehabilitation centers and radio shows.

Your fear is that non-whites might stop doing drugs and start doing books and higher education. You fear real competition. You fear not having enough non-whites to lock up. If no child got left behind, it would be a nightmare for you. Poverty is a mechanism you don't want to fix. I think you fear running out of bad guys. It's easier to let them kill each other and as long as they don't do it in your neighborhood, then it works in your favor. Sometimes the wrong people get killed but for the most part, the system's working just fine. If it wasn't, or in any way stepping on your profits, you would take care of it immediately.

You say you hate violent video games and rap music. You don't hate it that much because again, you have profit incentive. You don't hesitate to send America's young to Iraq to get slaughtered though because freedom isn't free. There's a price on it, there's a price on everything. You have so many ways to justify your profit and cowardice. Too bad you're not interested in spreading freedom and Democracy in America.

Poor people are great because they don't have many options besides the ones you provide. Don't you think it's about time you started thinking of the future and built installations in remote areas where the poor can live and be encouraged to breed prolifically to create future military personnel? You could start relocating people out of bad neighborhoods and sending them to the south specifically for this purpose. The annual welfare budget could be utilized for this. In one generation, you could have an almost completely non-white infantry. You can even breed for favorable traits and characteristics. They can be brave so whitey doesn't have to. Think about it, if you had a continuous supply of cannon fodder, you could take on any country at any time. Between the Axis of Evil™ and the Outposts of Tyranny™, there's going to be a lot of non-Christian ass to kick.

So let's get back to why I never stayed around for the beating of bad food, drugs and worthless culture. It's simple. I'm not weak. You're weak and full of fear and can only live in an environment of fear and dependency. You generate the fear and create dependency while you hold your myriad customers in great contempt as you stare down from the top of the moral mountaintop. Why would I want to be like you?

Thankfully, millions of us see you for what you are. You're worse than the ones you hold in contempt. So much worse.

How about this: Let's get rid of the Death Penalty™ and utilize mutilation as a deterrent. Deal drugs, lose a hand. It can be the hand of your choice. Rip off millions of people (like Bush's buds Fastow and Lay at Enron) and lose both. Could work. Let's test it in Utah.

I'll get all the drug dealers and corporate thieves together at Enron Field and from a well lit stage I'll yell, "You white motherfuckers! Throw your hands in the air!!" and they would throw their amputated hands in the air, which would excite the lions and we all could watch these pieces of shit get eaten.

Whitey, you corny bitch, watch out for those Ras Tafarians!! I hear they're teaming up with The Westsyde Lesbianz™. They're going to smoke out and go down on your daughter and the receptionist you're having the affair with.

Whitey, you can run from the truth but it'll find you and when it does, you'll get what you deserve. The streets will be slick with your blood and your wives will swing from branches like dem strange fruit.

You're my favorite can of beer to shake up and smash against the wall. Kill yourself tonight. Do it.

Song of the Solipsist

When I talk to you I turn to wood. I sit with the phone in my hand and lose it piece by piece. You shut me down and you have no idea. It's like I have two voices. One that screams without a sound and the other that takes over and does the talking. It's that one that never has the courage to say what it means. I hang up the phone, crushed. I know I'll never get it right.

You. Walking alone, anywhere. Looking up at the stars and thinking. Not looking at the stars like they would. Not thinking the things they would. Not like any of those bastards . . . Those idiots. They're not like you. Nothing like you. This fuckin' world, man . . . Always trying. Look at those stars. The poets will write it to pieces. Like it was some fucking dream. Dehumanized and no one can tell you a damn thing. Sidewalk under your feet. Looking at the stars. Thinking your thoughts. Fuck what any one of them think. They fill you with so much wasted time. You're cool. And the stars are all yours.

The less I carry around. The less I drag. I throw things out of my head all the time now. I see that a lot of the things that hung me up were things I was trying to hold onto. Things go where they go. People go away. You have to let them go. It all goes whichever way it's going to go. I see now that I cared too much about too much. Self-protection on my part. Kept me from getting to the point. I know the point. Ego shattering reality. That which can save you often disguises itself as the enemy. It's just another test.

A drawing of you embracing someone. The lines are smooth and warm. A drawing of you wrapping your arms around yourself. The lines are jagged. The portrait gives off sullen coldness. Black slashes on white paper. You in the corner of a bare, cold room. In your head. Wind screaming over rocks in a deep desert night. You're existing silently in the middle of a howling wind storm. So far out there. Broken beyond their understanding. So isolated and singular. That even language itself seems like an insult to feeling. And nothing they can say or do will bring you back all the way. You know.

Conflict. Trying to be happy is a lot more work than I had thought. Trying to get along with myself. A wind sprint on a ten mile trail of sniper infested tree line.

0450 hrs. New York City. Can't sleep. The sounds of traffic have died down. There's nothing to distract me from myself. Trying hard not to sink into the normal depressed state. I know there's no sinking to be done. I'm here. I have been struggling. I just want to stand up. I want to get out of the hole. I want to see more than nothing in all their eyes. Trying to get myself motivated to do something. To care about someone. I wasn't always like this. It feels like I got thrown off a train moving through the night. I was fine until then. I pick myself up and look around. I don't recognize anything. The fall knocked so much out of my head but I know enough to know I'm empty and lost. It's hard to give a damn about anything these days. I don't know what I'm going to do with myself. I spend entire days in low level panic. Everything makes me mad and confused. I thought I was over things and I see I'm not over much. Unfinished, never started. Panic in the middle of the night.

I try to keep myself steady. Tonight is like many nights I have gone through. I'm in England and it's near three in the morning. Another night I have woken up in panic feeling like dying. Confused and alone in a hotel room. A way to feel better escapes me. I am too cynical for my own good. It's the beginning of the year. I don't feel like moving. Don't feel like doing anything. I don't miss anyone. I think of violence and Death. What I should have done. All that crap. You know the rest. You knew it from the first line on. You got me again.

She clings to me and I want to think that it's special. People should find each other I think. It's some of the only real magic left. But I know better. She buries her head into my neck because she's trying to get away from some old boyfriend, her father, some rapist, some dream. She's not trying to get closer to me. I try to break through my flesh and go inside her, not to be closer, but to get away from pain and the vacancy of my life. We are silently escaping, tightly clenched, limbs intertwined, distant. The bed fills with blood and we are awash in sorrow and fear. We cling tighter. The past kills everything. I don't believe in romance or love at first sight. I believe in mutual desperation.

I'll never escape you. No matter where I am I know you're watching. I feel your eyes on my back when I fuck. I know why people kill their parents.

So what am I supposed to do? All that old shit? Write you crazy letters all night long? Think about you all the time? Say that I'm tearing myself apart over you? No. Maybe I'm getting too old for it. I just can't make myself care enough about you. Or anyone else. It just could be that I'm free. What do I do now?

Saw you for the first time in years. You tried to touch me. I went rigid. I felt the anger rise. All the nights of helpless idiotic frustration. All the thoughts of you. Came back like they never left. I looked at your face and listened to your voice. It made me think of every thing that ever held me back. Your friendliness made me cold. You asked me if I had any loves in my life. No, fuck no. You try to get close to me all you get is cold. All you get is distance. All you get is a dead man. All you get is the heartbreak of ruined expectation.

The devastation of willful damage. I said I don't like anyone being close to me. There's been too many people like you in my life. Now why don't you just go on your fucking way. Before I make you cry in front of all of these people. You want someone nice then go talk to the guy not shot full of empty night holes. All I'll do is rip you apart.

Turn off the light. Tell me things that won't make me scream. Slowly. Make me come to life again. It's been so long. They drag the shadow man into the light. He damn near turned to ash. That's me. Hold the carcass close to your body. Tell me things that won't make me lose my mind . I don't want to tell you my truth: You're eyes are the only way out I see. Shake some sense into me. I've been stupid for so long. Not my fault all the way. I had help. There's always someone to show you to the bottom.

Every time I think the world has come to an end, it keeps on crawling. I figured that the sheer weight of all the drug dealers on the corners would make the land sink into the sea. I walked by them tonight here in Atlanta. Looking distant and full of thought, they stood next to every phone booth for blocks. I lost my will to eat and turned back to the hotel. Walked past them all again. Waited to sink with them. Nothing happened. That's the fucked up thing. Nothing happens until a nightmare erupts. You feel the gun's barrel at the back of your head. You can smell instinct. It rises off the flesh when the body is getting ready to fold. Paranoia all the time. Kills you slowly. The hardest boss there is.

I saved you a few nightmares. No lady. I don't want to know. Don't want to touch. Don't want to fuck you. You think it's rejection. I'm doing you a favor.

Stretched faced man. Allows the sidewalks to make him insane. Believes all the love songs. Sweats and silently kills. Mentally murders flesh. Cripples himself. Staggers from too much poison. Please take the pain away. Don't let me lose control. The bullet threw the brains to the west wall.

Instead of the drama. Leave. Leave like the others did. I don't have a heart to break. You leave, you stay. It's all the same to me. Fuck it. Just leave.

The snow truck scrapes the street outside. 2:13 a.m. Ottawa Canada Holiday Inn room #439. Where do you go with your heart's wild music?. The hollowing dull roar of strangers. Lines of hands. Loneliness as a weakly flapping appendage. Obsolete. Won't be included on the next model. What has happened to me?

Don't cut me. I'm all grown up now. I can do it myself.

Not born abusive. But good at repeating the steps. Knowledge beyond knowledge. You get so involved with the language of pain, its storage and release, you think it's in your blood. But it's not. It's lessons learned and actions repeated blending in well with the dark tree line of total obscenity.

I will always disappoint you. Always break you into pieces, leave you waiting and hanging scattered. Then I will forget you. I will always waste your time. You will hate me. My calm indifference, the way I will effortlessly distance myself from you and act as if nothing had ever happened between us will infuriate you. Because to me, nothing did. I'm one of those dead men. Beyond sickness, hope and all that other shit.

My room as hotel, everything as temporary. Every possession thought of only as a rental. People thought of only as potential killers or interrogators. If I can be always ready to lose it all then I won't get hurt again. I wasted a lot of time waiting on people. It was my own fault. I think of all the time I spent trying to know women. I was doing someone else's trip. The only times I felt anything were the times I temporarily convinced myself it was real but I know that it never was. It was only me lying to myself. Something I wanted it to be, someone else's idea. So I stripped it away, I tore off the skin that had been suffocating me. It fell to the floor. I was very alone after that. I look at myself in my brain and I am ashamed at the way I was. There was never a chance. How embarrassing. Who the hell did I think I was? Someone trying to survive? I didn't even have that much sense, it hurts to know that survival for me was accidental and sheer luck, never my own will. It's raining outside tonight. Rain is something that I miss. I used to like going out in the rain. I didn't mind walking home when it was raining. Raining in LA, what a joke. All the syringes and bullet casings go into the gutter. All the sad stories slip into the sewer. All the trails of all the swan song bands and all the fakes who got slaughtered on the streets. Can you imagine anyone living out their lives here? Earlier tonight I saw the whores all bunched at the corner with the drug dealers. I looked through the windshield and thought of the streets of my youth and the walks I wasn't afraid to take back then. That was a long time ago and I'm not supposed to care about that shit anymore right? If I hold onto things then I have no chance. If I hold onto anything except myself all I'll ever do is wallow. I treat this room like a hotel. I treat this whole set up as temporary. I don't take anyone in close. All I know is that if I don't keep moving I'll crash. None of them are close to me. If they try they get pushed back. I am alone in the room, in all rooms, all the time. The only time I get messed up is when I attach to anyone or anything. Less people I keep in touch with the better. I am alone on the planet. I just keep to myself. I don't want anyone to know me and I don't want to know anyone. That's why I tell the truth. I want to get it all out of me so at the end there will be nothing. They'll come in and try to take something from me and they'll go away mad because there will be nothing more to take. I'll say ha! I already got rid of it. They'll get nothing.

Home tank. Sitting in the room. No one calls, nothing happens. I've been here a few days. I'll be gone in a few more. It's night time. LA's outside. Fuck it, I'm not going out there. Bullet streets. All those run down looking moth-erfuckers. Stupid kill you men. Strange mouthed and dislocated. Nothing to live for. So-go-ahead-go-for-your-piece kind of looks in their eyes. Standing around. Blocking the sidewalks. Detouring this air. Vacantly confronting. Unknowingly challenging. No character. Nothing. Except empty hallway I'll-live-the-rest-of-my-life-here I-know-guys-who-got-killed I've-done-time day to day paranoia to panic to twitching life. No. I can't deal with guys like that. It's like getting mad at a shadow. What are you going to do to a killer who died when he was 12, who is now 26 and doesn't care? One of these days they'll scrape a body off the street. I'll look at the face and see myself. Another dead man. Stricken. Lungs full of blood poison. We'll laugh at our decay. We'll call it something else. Then we'll lie down, pull the dust over us like a blanket, admit that the relentless city ripped us up and broke us like a cheap reproduction of something wonderful.

I get used to throwing parts of myself away. The days pass and I realize I have cored myself out again and become a deep stranger. A time comes when I need help. I'm not there for myself. That's bad because I never look to any of these fuckers to help me. I can sit in some backstage dump and feel parts of myself starve to Death. It's no big deal. It really isn't.

You're not born a loser. You work at it. Failure after failure. Soon you're pulling off great ones with ease. You get so good. People think you're born to lose. You see them go. Losers always get there first and stay the longest. You see them moving fast. They know that they don't have much time before they get caught. They are the most honest with women. They're the ones that get hurt the most. They fall for every sucker punch in the book. They always try to do the right thing. They always get taken out at the knees by some guy who tries half as hard. A guy who never sweats details. You always can spot the loser. He always has that look on his face. Like he's learning the same thing. For the millionth time. For all of his honesty and pain, you hate him. You want him to keep losing. He makes you feel better about yourself. He makes all your meager accomplishments seem like monumental feats instead of what they really are. The don't see themselves in you. You see yourself in them. You avoid losers. They know too much.

I look at you and I know I'm not wrong. I am drawn to you. The attraction is pure as dirt. I claw myself from the inside. I know already. Too far away. Too much damage done. If things were different. I could show you something besides obsessed fury. You're beautiful. No one knows it more than I do. It's hard to stand and watch from a distance. The fact that I wouldn't know what to do anyway makes it hurt all the more.

I would tell you everything. I would give you all I have if I could trust you. If you wouldn't think I was crazy. If you wouldn't freak out and leave me while I was freaking out and leaving you. I'm scared of going far away while sitting in front of you. I'm terrified of terrifying you. I don't want to hurt anyone. I know I do though. I'm walking dead. I don't care about most things anymore. I hurt people's feelings all the time. They ask how I could say something like that to someone else. How I can be so cold. I don't feel. I don't know the damage I do. I think I might be in the wrong business. Truth has never been valued in my profession. A lot of them just want everyone else to like them. They'll do whatever it takes. They really don't care. I think that more cruel in a way. They are adoration hoarders. They go door to door collecting power. They say that they don't care what anyone thinks. They spend more time thinking about you than you ever will about them. I always saw that as an insecurity and a reminder of myself.

I am dead right now. I am on auto pilot. There's a way I've found to be around and not be at the same time. I live in the bottoms of my eyes. I figure if I'm not around they can't bother me. When they call my name I keep walking like I'm dead. I am and I can't break through to someone else. I have tried in the last 19 months and nothing happens so I know what my deal is now. I just hang out, check the pain levels. Earn my existence and wait around. Their praise means nothing to me. I just nod and keep looking out the window. At this point I'm damned. Locked into a stare down with the Abyss. I'm losing. I'm becoming filled with emptiness. Soon there will be no more. I wonder what I'll be like then?

Silently I wait for the end. I am proud of my silence. I do my best to maintain it. Even when I want to get out of this room. I know the bottom line. They'll fuck me up. In a dishonorable fashion. So I stay here and wait, try not to be pathetic.

I tried to meet this woman a few months ago. Now I am full of regret. I never should have said a word. When I think of the way I have humiliated myself yet again. It seems that's the only thing I'm good at. Besides taking pain and holding my small piece of ground.

I keep my mouth shut. It makes me stronger. All my failures have occurred when I tried to interact with others. This room makes more sense than all the wild and stupid explanations. All the time wasting nights staring at nothing in the darkness. Filling myself with frustration thinking about them. Always them. Silence and solitude is better.

Wandering ghost. I have no ambition. It was destroyed by my resolve. I have no ego. My insecurity killed itself. I am dead. I am unstoppable.

When I'm lucky. Moments of nothing sometimes stretch into hours. When I'm empty. Thoughtless. I'm ok. I can breathe without thinking about not breathing. Saving me from the rest of my allotted time. When I know just enough to remember nothing.

Silent Zero. Remain underneath them all. Feel less worthy. Know you must work harder than the rest. And that you will never get as far. To think that the struggle is over is to succumb. To rest is to lose. Don't rely on them for anything.

I have no peace of mind. I have no inner calm. I see why I do what I do. I am in constant conflict with myself. I like the weights for the pain. I like music because it's the sound of things flying apart. I want to tear myself to pieces. It makes sense. I see why people kill. I understand why they kill themselves. Life doesn't move fast enough for some.

Tonight under clear skies with no stars I walk alone. I explore the planes of solitude amongst loud groups of fast talking humans. Language. Shrill, roaring and meaningless to me. September in New York. I walk carefully to avoid recognition. The worst is when they touch me. Slap me on the back and yell in my ear. I go out late to avoid them. I have all the unpopular streets memorized. It occurred to me the other night that I'm an outcast. Walking on the outskirts everywhere I go. Avoiding the eyes. Wilting under their stares Not doing so well with the whole thing.

My main goal is to stay alive. To keep fooling myself into hanging around. To keep getting up every day. Right now I live without inspiration. I go day to day and do the work because it's all I know. I know that if I keep moving I stand a chance. I must keep myself going until I find a reason to live. I need one so bad. On the other hand maybe I don't. Maybe it's all bullshit. Nothing I knew from my old life can help me here. Most of the things that I believed turned out to be useless. Appendages from someone else's life.

Everything I have I would give to not know what I know. To not feel emptiness as my constant companion. To not look into this room and be reminded why I'm in it. I'm not getting enough air. The room feels so small all of a sudden. It's pathetic to be this lonely and know it. To keep breathing. To be silent and alone. And to know.

It wouldn't be so bad if I wasn't in this all by myself. It would be good to have someone to look over to. Someone to dodge the arrows with. They come with all kinds of weapons these days. Fangs, stinging venom, slings, thorns, the works. They say: We know you're one of the good guys. But we're going to ruin you anyway, watch. So at this late hour, alone in this room, this is what occurs to me. All I know is I'm getting out before they get tired of letting me up for air. I never underestimate them in any way.

Sometimes it's not catastrophic. Sometimes you only come to the bottom of your coffee cup. Sometimes you have a good day. No one wants to know. No one wants to tell you about theirs either. You might somehow take it. Turn it against them. See the flaw. You always tell them the whole thing sucks. It keeps you alive. They figure if you're out there having a rotten time, everything's fine and you're doing your part. No one will ever try to take your bad times away from you but they'll come swarming for your happiness.

I would be a liar if I said I wasn't impressed. Or at least terrified and sick of the world outside my window. From my view I almost see the street. I can't get the window to open very far. The safety bars get in the way. Well past midnight, they're still out there screaming. I'm in here hiding, with all my unimpressed, alone in my room with my uncaring. Tired of the idiots. Tired of being tired of them all the time. It's work, man. The man with the gun in his pants. One who doesn't give a fuck. He walks by, checks the bars on my window. Is he a thief? A prison guard? It's too late for the humans. We're just hanging out waiting. The government will give us the right disease to die from any time now. Until then just keep choking on the poison. Keep tripping on the violence. Remain numb to the headlines. Ignore the cruelty you inflict on all those strangers. That's all they are. You might as well become everything you hate.

Craving extinction. Willing myself into nothing. It's sometimes better than being so aware. Aware to the point where it all hurts. Where it all makes you feel like the girl who called last night, wanting to die. So desperate, she called the office on a Saturday looking for me. I listened to her describe horror alleys of anguish I knew so well. At times she could barely get the words out. Sometimes I try to think of a nothing so big it will eclipse all the poison in my brain. A thought so overwhelming and black it will knock me into extinction for awhile until I can catch my breath.

Sunset on the Vet. Requiem for the mortal. Victim of the crime. Bearer of Horror's weight. Sayer of the unspeakable. Witness of the act. Darkness is what I know. Everything and everyone closing in. All the hands are choking. I don't ask for help. I don't believe I fell off, fell out of bounds. Everything you say and do, so what. Fuck it.

Good morning and here's some napalm. Your generation is invisible. It's been no time at all and you're already extinct. One big scream with no mouth. You'll pay double. You'll pay endlessly. You might get murdered or audited in the process.

After a while all the pieces fell to the bottom. The roar in his ears stopped and darkness settled in. He lived alone in the house. He kept the shutters drawn. No one heard his screams, his curse-filled lectures to the walls. No one wondered, no one knew. No relatives. No one. The shadows knew him well but weren't interested. The dust wasn't either. Time kept watch but eventually left. He saw what he saw. It was all he could do to contain himself. He could not identify with anyone. He knew that he knew. Life looked elsewhere and moved on.

She's beautiful. She never judges me. She understands me completely. She heals my wounds. I could look into her eyes for days. I think of her. Every time I fuck you.

I see it now. You're full of lies. You're a bag of leeching nights. You should find some stupid animal to fuck you. Chain some stupid motherfucker to a post in your basement. Kick him in the side when you want to get serviced. Maybe get two stupid animals. It's never enough is it? The words fall dead from your mouth. You wish you could attract with something besides the obvious. But you don't pay it too much mind. Because the obvious gets you serviced. But it doesn't get me.

I wish you could make me feel like living. I wish you meant something to me. I touch you and feel the wall rise up. You touch me and I feel nothing. I don't tell you because I don't want to hurt you. I don't want to hurt anyone. I don't even want to hurt myself anymore.

For a moment I almost felt safe. I almost felt alive. I could feel your warmth on me. Your hair brushing my chest. I almost closed my eyes. But I couldn't because it was then you could have stabbed me. Sleep comes best alone. Behind a triple locked hotel room door checked in under a different name.

I keep turning inward. Keep staying alone. Keep denying myself. Take the pain. Keep taking the pain. Don't lose consciousness. Stay with it. Why? Because it's better than listening to you.

The guy yells MTV! Yo, MTV! I seen you man! I sit up on my hind legs and say thank you.

Touch me so I can remember how alone I am. Stay here. Re-enforce the futility. Tell me your secrets. Remind me of how we're all the same. Hurt me. Make me see that you're human.

There's some things we're not going to discuss. I'll go so far with you and then you're alone with me in front of you, staring mutely through you like some stupid animal.

Open your arms to hold me. Open your eyes to see me. Open your mouth to kiss me. Open. Open everything. You come over here. I'll go over there. We'll run around. We'll braid our secrets. We'll always know. We'll never tell.

If I never see you again. I will train my thoughts. I will make them strong so they will protect you from any distance. If I never hear your voice again, I will remember the sound of you calling my name. If you never touch me again, I will remember the feeling of being whole so loneliness will not recognize me.

Fuck it. I'm grounded deep in the anti thought. The pure-pure is mine only as this night burns. I've not grown tired of punching the sidewalk with my fists. I'm tired of holding back. How can I not hate you? How can I not be disgusted? All the shit you get away with. This age is too weak. The words no longer hold me. I don't want to ignore you. I want to fuck you up. Vulgar. No matter what you do. You cannot stop your self mutilation. You're turning insect mutant contemporary auto-tragic. Standing on your hind legs as you twitch. Humanity back burner music exploding your ears with man-made pavement under your feet. "Look, I really want to have sex with you. I know it's good for my cardio." An almost model. Another human speeding failure. To wade through this decadent swill is an endless insult to my existence. You wonder why there's human monsters. You wonder why people get killed for no reason. I don't. Because there's always a reason. A human mind compressed into an amoral diamond mine. Enough is enough. I've got proof.

I want to be filled with stupidity right now. I want to believe in dreams. I want to believe in you and your face. I need to be filled with the non screaming thought. Shot in the head. With a torment destroying bullet that does not kill. Love blunts the pain. Throws cataracts across the eyes. Gives the illusion of strength. I need it now. I need some word to repeat. A picture to kiss. An overheard shot of me shows a man flailing as he drops straight into darkness. No sound is heard.

I never wanted skin this thick. Sometimes I surprise myself. The things that still come out of my mouth. And the things that I never say. I never thought I would see so much of you. I never knew I would have to see so deeply. You become what you see. You are your experiences. I have become cities. Thousands of screaming nights. All the violence. I have not risen above it. I have disappeared into it. From now on it's pointed and undercover. Full of paranoia and neon lit fear. I am working on the monster. It will be my life's work. Every night I build the creature. Who will die when I die. More pain and more fury. Watching the criminals. At one time I did want something from you.

To understand perfection you must have a thorough understanding of imperfection. I see it in the rearview mirror. Looking back at how it could have been if I didn't get in the way of myself and run it over. Know what you want. Don't stop until you're dead. This is all I have. I know that there's nothing else to do with myself. My decisions are as easy as turning something on or off. What you think doesn't have anything to do with it.

My longing throws itself out of an NYC apartment window. So desperate to get away from me. Can't take the smallness of this room. Past two in the morning and the heat is surging. Sirens and traffic. My body sticks to itself. I am trying to get to sleep before dawn. Last night a woman was in this room with me. The night was fine. The morning was strange. Strangers adultly covering their desperation. Knowing it didn't work. Knowing it didn't stop the loneliness. Knowing it never pulls its spikes out of your back. Knowing but going on anyway.

Australian sun settles to steel grey. Streets are abandoned. The bars are half filled. The old men on their stools are quiet. Their movements are slow and rustling. Approaching death is quiet. Sounds like leaves blowing across a lost city sidewalk. It moves in slow and has no face. I walk by and look in, flattened by the endless sky and the descending night. The road ahead of me is an exhausted exhale. Devoid of drama and emotion. Absolute truth waits for me. Somehow.